SELECTED POEMS

OF

JEHUDAH HALEVI

EDITED BY

HEINRICH BRODY

THE JEWISH PUBLICATION
SOCIETY OF AMERICA
Philadelphia

ADVERTISEMENT

The present Series of JEWISH CLASSICS was projected in continuation of the previous publication of the English Translation of the HOLY SCRIPTURES—the greatest classic of Hebrew literature and of all times.

When the New Translation of the Scriptures was approaching completion, the late Jacob H. Schiff, through whose munificence the publication of that translation was rendered possible, further proposed to the Jewish Publication Society of America that they should issue a representative selection of the various classes of literature produced by Jewish writers after the close of the Biblical Canon, and for that purpose placed a fund at the disposal of the Society.

In the deed of gift of Mr. Schiff, which was intended to make the present Series possible, a Committee was named by him consisting of the following:

Dr. Solomon Schechter, Chairman
Dr. Cyrus Adler, Vice-Chairman
Rev. Dr. H. G. Enelow
Prof. Israel Friedlaender
Rev. Dr. Kaufmann Kohler
Prof. Alexander Marx
Rev. Dr. F. de Sola Mendes

1

Rev. Dr. David Philipson
Rev. Dr. Samuel Schulman
The Hon. Mayer Sulzberger

Later the Committee was increased by the addition of Prof. Louis Ginzberg, Prof. Jacob Z. Lauterbach, and Prof. Henry Malter. Upon the death of Dr. Schechter, Dr. Cyrus Adler was elected Chairman, and Prof. Israel Davidson was named to succeed Prof. Friedlaender. The Committee has since been deprived of the aid of Judge Sulzberger, who passed away on April 20, 1923.

The plan of the Series, however, was outlined during the Chairmanship of our distinguished colleague, the eminent scholar, Dr. Solomon Schechter.

The first principle adopted was that in all cases in which a Hebrew text was extant, it was to be printed along with the English translation, and that an endeavor should be made to present a critical text based not only upon previous editions, but also upon the available manuscripts. For this purpose manuscripts have been photographed in the libraries of England, Italy, Germany, Austria, and Hungary— wherever important manuscripts bearing upon the Series were to be found—and the Committee feel that in offering this Series they are not only making accessible to English readers some of the treasures of Jewish literature, but are adding to Jewish scholarship by presenting carefully edited texts, which they hope will become the standard texts of the Jewish Classics.

In giving the original Hebrew text the Committee have been able to add a feature which was absent in the publication of the translation of the Scriptures, the English text of which was published without the original Hebrew. This was not due to any desire on the part of the Board in charge to substitute the English text for the original; but the demand for an English version on the part of English-speaking Jews was so urgent, and the facilities in the United States for printing Hebrew at the time so meager, that the Board felt any further delay of a work that had been anxiously expected for twenty years would be inadvisable. It is the hope of the Jewish Publication Society to publish, when its opportunities permit, the Hebrew text of the Bible, side by side with the translation.

The Committee were limited in the preparation of the Series by the amount of the fund, which, though most generous, could not provide for a complete presentation of the Jewish Classics, which might well cover hundreds of volumes.

They therefore decided, in the first instance, to omit, by reason of their availability in the English language, certain works which would otherwise naturally be expected to appear in such a Series. This is notably the case in regard to two great philosophical works—the *Kuzari* of Jehudah Halevi, which has been translated into English by Doctor Hartwig Hirschfeld, and the *Guide of the Perplexed* of Moses Maimonides, which has an English version at the hands of the late Doctor Michael Friedländer. Similarly two great names like those of Flavius Josephus and Philo of Alexandria, although rightfully belonging to a series of Jewish Classics, were not included because we were given to understand that they had already been selected for publication in the Loeb Classical Library.

The Committee deemed it necessary to limit the Series to about 25 volumes, and they will endeavor to include in this number representative works of the various classes of Jewish literature under the headings of Apocrypha and Pseudepigrapha, Mishnah, Talmud, Midrash, Codes, Hebrew Poetry, Philosophy, Ethics, Mysticism, History, Epistles, Travels, Homiletics, and Folklore.

The Series was inaugurated with a selection from the religious poems of Solomon Ibn Gabirol, edited by Professor Israel Davidson, and put into English verse by Mr. Israel Zangwill. The present, the second volume of the Series, is based largely upon the critical text of the *Diwan* of Jehudah Halevi, prepared by the distinguished Rabbi Heinrich Brody of Prag, and published under the auspices of the Mekize Nirdamim Society. Doctor Brody has graciously permitted the use of these selections, and has made certain alterations in his published text, and supplied several notes for the present volume. The translation is due to Mrs. Nina Salaman, who has for a decade been the medium through which many English readers have had glimpses into medieval Jewish poetry. Her *Songs of Exile*, published in 1901 under the name of Nina Davis, have become known to thousands of readers. It is a source of profound gratification to the Committee to be able to offer the work of this gifted lady in the present Series.

While the body of her translation has been done in free verse, she has made several additional translations, in stricter form, and with rhyme, which are printed together toward the end of the volume.

ADVERTISEMENT

The Committee trust that this Series will awaken the interest and command the support of those who feel the obligation to see to it that the Jewish Classics, which, with few exceptions, have been unknown to English readers, shall come into their own, and take their rightful place among the classic literatures of all peoples.

September, 1924

The SCHIFF LIBRARY
of JEWISH CLASSICS

SELECTED POEMS

OF

JEHUDAH HALEVI

TRANSLATED INTO ENGLISH

BY

NINA SALAMAN

CHIEFLY FROM THE CRITICAL TEXT

EDITED BY

HEINRICH BRODY, Ph.D.

PHILADELPHIA

The Jewish Publication Society of America

1924

מחברת משירי

יהודה בן שמואל הלוי

נערכו והוגהו

על ידי

חיים בראדי

רב הכולל בעיר פראג

עם תרגום אנגלי

מאת

נינה אשת ר' נתן בן מאיר שלמה

פילאדלפיא

החברה היהודית להוצאת ספרים אשר באמריקה

תרפ"ד

PRINTED AT
THE JEWISH PUBLICATION SOCIETY PRESS
PHILADELPHIA, PENNA.

CONTENTS

[1]Rhymed Version, p. 151
[2]Rhymed Version, p. 157.

[1]Rhymed Version, p. 159.
[2]Rhymed Version, p. 161.

IV. DEVOTIONAL POEMS

[1]Rhymed Version, p. 162.
[2]Rhymed Version, p. 164.

[1]Rhymed Version, p. 165.

[2]Rhymed Version, p. 166.　　[3]Rhymed Version, p. 167.

[4]Rhymed Version, p. 168.　　[5]Rhymed Version, p. 170.

[6]Rhymed Version, p. 172.　　[7]Rhymed Version, p. 174.

RHYMED TRANSLATIONS

אֲנִי כִנּוֹר לְשִׁירָיִךְ

"*I am a harp for thy songs*"

INTRODUCTION

THE GIFT of song, cherished and tended as
it was by the Spanish Jews of the Middle Ages,
reached its highest development in the poems of
Jehudah ben Samuel Halevi, born, as is now gen-
erally accepted, in Toledo in 1086, the story of
whose life as physician, philosopher and poet
has come down to us in but slight fragments,
and ends vaguely among the mists of tradition.
In the disturbed atmosphere of the Spain of his
day, Castile lay under the comparatively mild
sway of the Catholic King Alfonso VI. Per-
secution was as yet occasional, and only burst
into flames if the favour shown to the Jews was
considered by their ill-wishers to be unduly
great. Judging from Jehudah Halevi's letters
to his friends, his life passed in serving the people
of Toledo, where many of his years were spent,
as their much sought-after and hard-worked
physician; and one suspects his profession to
have been a rather burdensome incident in
his life, while his whole heart and soul were
consumed in the pursuit, as he says, of the
"fount of living waters."

Yet we must be on our guard against taking too literally his depreciation of the medical art. He was equally outspoken against metaphysics in his treatise on the Philosophy of Judaism, the *Kitab al-Khazari*, his one great Arabic work. The truth is that, even more than Spinoza, Jehudah Halevi was "God-intoxicated" or, to use Heine's phrase, "God-kissed". God, not the physician, was to him the Healer; God, not human reason, was the source of truth. The physician was but God's servant, and by Him endowed with such gift of healing as he possessed.

From evidence to be found in the poems, we know that their author was bound to Spain by the presence and love of his one daughter and her little son, Jehudah, [1] as well as by the minor ties of memory [2] and by many friendships. But one love was to be conquered by the power of another, and we find the poet at the age of fifty years journeying forth on the perilous seas to seek the still more greatly beloved land of his fathers. Heine detected this love and this longing, but it needs not the insight of a Heine to perceive it—the most casual reader of Halevi's poems realizes that the poet's soul

[1] See latter half of poem No. 11 in the Selection.
[2] See No. 13 in the Selection.

is bound up with his love for his people and their lost land. It was about the year 1141 that he set out on his journey to Palestine, cheerfully facing the hardships of the way and the stormy seas, and making songs about them as he went. Not the least of his inheritance from the sweet singer of Israel was his descriptive power. He pictures storm and landscape with the vivid touch of actuality. His praise of nature is no literary trick, we catch the genuine notes of a nature-lover. As evening falls and the stars come out, he writes of sea and sky:

> They are like two seas bound up together;
> And between them is my heart—a third sea
> Lifting up ever anew my waves of praise.[1]

So we can trace his steps from Spain to Alexandria, the Jews everywhere giving him a friendly reception, and strongly but vainly urging him to remain with them and to discontinue his perilous pilgrimage. Further we hear of his passing up the Nile and visiting the community at Cairo and Damietta, and he is known to have touched Tyre and Damascus. But after his arrival in Palestine, definite reports fade into rumours. Tradition tells us that he was ridden down and slain by an Arab

---

[1] Last lines of No. 5 in Selection.

when at last he reached his goal and was sing-
ing his great Song to Zion by the ruins he
had longed to see. Certain it is, however, that
many of its lines must have been written while
his desire to reach Jerusalem was yet but a
dream. His poem reaches its appointed end
in his ardent confidence that the age-long hope
of his suffering people will find its fulfilment.

The poet Swinburne has written a few lines
in a poem called "The Triumph of Time",
about another singer of the Middle Ages—
lines which make one think equally of the life,
the love, and the death of Jehudah Halevi:

> There lived a singer in France of old
>   By the tideless dolorous midland sea.
> In a land of sand and ruin and gold
>   There shone one woman, and none but she.
> And finding life for her love's sake fail,
> Being fain to see her, he bade set sail,
> Touched land, and saw her as life grew cold,
>   And praised God, seeing; and so died he.

The French singer loved and sought the lady
of his dreams; but she whom the Rabbi loved,
as Heine has said—"her name was Jerusalem"

Jehudah Halevi has attained the highest honour
to which a writer can aspire—the esteem of
his peers. Harizi, the Hebrew poet-critic of
a generation near his own, describes him as

supremely inimitable, as one who "broke into
the treasure-house of song", and who, going
out again, "shut the gate behind him". His
love-songs, his prayers, his epistles are all alike
"drawn from the Holy Spirit". Some six
centuries later, when Herder—a philosopher-poet
like Jehudah Halevi himself—composed his epoch-
making treatise on the Spirit of Hebrew Poetry,
his model (so he himself recorded) in great
passages of dialogue was "not Plato but Jehudah
Halevi." And Heine has immortalised his own
appreciation of our poet in several famous
stanzas of his *Romanzero*.

Hence we ought not to assent without res-
ervation to a judgment passed by Joseph Jacobs
in his brilliant essay on Jehudah Halevi. He
there draws an interesting and just distinction
between poetic *form* and poetic *force*. Brown-
ing, he points out, had great poetic force, but
little poetic form; Swinburne, a master of form,
lacked force. As applied to Yannai and Kalir
and others of that earlier school, this distinction
is perhaps relevant. But it is not profitable
to say of them, still less of Jehudah Halevi, that
"they worked in a medium that did not admit
of great poetic form". If defect there were, it
was in the mediary not in the medium; in the
hand, not in the instrument. In Kalir—to cite

a few lines from the opening of his Piyut on
the Dew—force is more apparent than form:

טַל תֵּן לִרְצוֹת אַרְצֶךָ

שִׁיתֵנוּ בְרָכָה בְּדִיצֶךָ

רוֹב דָּגָן וְתִירוֹשׁ בְּהַפְרִיצֶךָ

קוֹמֵם עִיר בָּהּ חֶפְצֶךָ

בְּטָל

Israel Zangwill has thus rendered these lines:

Dew, precious dew, unto Thy land forlorn!
·Pour out our blessing in Thy exultation,
To strengthen us with ample wine and corn
And give Thy chosen city safe foundation
In Dew.

Here the thought is impressive, and the Hebraic
conception of the Dew as the reviver of earth
and soul is well developed as the *piyut* proceeds.
But the Hebrew verses jingle harshly. Is the
fault in the medium? Contrast these lines
with two verses from an early song of Jehudah
Halevi's in praise of Jerusalem:

קִרְיָה לְמֶלֶךְ רָב   יָפֶה נוֹף מְשׂוֹשׂ תֵּבֵל

מִפַּאֲתֵי מַעֲרָב   לָךְ נִכְסְפָה נַפְשִׁי

כִּי אֶזְכְּרָה קֶדֶם   הֲמוֹן רַחֲמַי נִכְמָר

וּנְוֵךְ אֲשֶׁר חָרָב   כְּבוֹדָךְ אֲשֶׁר גָּלָה

Beautiful height! the whole world's gladness!
O great King's city, mountain blest!

My soul is yearning unto thee—is yearning
  From limits of the West.

The torrents heave from depths of passion,
  At memory of thine olden state:
The glory of thee, borne away to exile,
  Thy dwelling desolate.

Thus is force wedded to a beauty of form
which must give pause to all depreciation of
the medium. For in these Hebrew lines of
our poet, it is not merely the elegiac sentiment
that moves us; we are charmed equally by their
lyric grace.

Moreover, that Jehudah Halevi was a stylist
as well as a man of ideas, is shown by the fact
that, while his Hebrew is easily understood,
he is not easy to translate. This difficulty
sometimes arises from the exigencies of rhyme.
We are not attempting in this Introduction
to analyze Jehudah Halevi's poetical schemes, or
to discuss their relation to real or assumed Arabic
parallels. It must suffice to state that some of
these poetical schemes are very intricate, and
recondite terms are occasionally chosen, not
because those terms are the most suitable, but
because the rhyme, the acrostic, or the metre
demands them. The translator must sometimes
ignore these enforced expressions, just as as-

sonances and alliterations must sometimes be abandoned as irreproducible. But the difficulty of exact translation mostly arises from a deeper cause, accruing not from the poet's failures but from his successes, from his inspired choice of words, from his mastery of style. Perhaps we ought not to describe Jehudah Halevi's Hebrew as easy. His simplicity is delusive. But is not this true of all great lyrists? Masters of song use the one right word, for which there is no equivalent in their own or in any other language. This mastery is not consistent, and the greatest poets have their intermittences. Jehudah Halevi is no exception. But Heine describes him, and in the main with verity, as one of the aristocracy of letters, possessing that grace, in virtue of which "they who have it cannot sin, not in verse nor yet in prose". This quality is seen also in Ibn Gabirol, but in Jehudah Halevi more organically. Both, for instance, repeatedly employ biblical phraseology. But with Ibn Gabirol the employment is that of an artist, with Jehudah Halevi of a musician. One sees Ibn Gabirol using a text for a final touch of shape and colour; one hears Jehudah Halevi working his texts into the very substance of his harmony. From the *Royal Crown* one might, without much mutilation of the structure, omit from each stanza the closing citation, artistic coping stones though they are. One could not discard Jehudah Halevi's biblical allusions from a Zion Ode without leaving the music incomplete or even discordant.

The poet's gift of grace, his inability to sin, whether in verse or in prose, is shown again in the work already mentioned, the *Kitab al-Khazari*. Dr. Hirschfeld, its translator from the Arabic, well says, this is a "book for the people". It "contains sufficient attractive and instructive material even for readers who would skip the more abstruse passages". The treatise, a series of five dialogues, is romantically framed in the medieval story of the King of the Khazars, the royal convert to Judaism who came under the wings of the Shekhinah after doubt and controversy. There is much in these dialogues on technical topics; astronomy and philology, among other serious subjects, play their part. But, regarded as a whole, the *Khazari* is as much a poem as are its author's poems themselves. At all events, Jehudah Halevi takes the poet's view of Judaism and of the Jews. Israel is the heart of mankind, filling the same function in the world at large as does the heart in the body of man. This is Halevi's epigram and text. Taking into account particularly the first of the dialogues we might almost argue that the poet possessed dramatic gifts, though he appears never to have attempted to write a formal drama.

Our reference to the Khazari reminds us of yet another of Jehudah Halevi's contradictions, a contradiction which, however, we must not take too seriously. Let us listen to part of a conversation between the Khazar King and his Rabbi interlocutor, as rendered into English by Dr. H. Hirschfeld. Discussing with the Rabbi the qualities of the Hebrew language, the King of the Khazars remarks:

"Thou wilt only succeed in placing it thus on an equality with other languages. But where is its pre-eminence? Other languages surpass it in songs metrically constructed and set to music."

The Rabbi: "It is obvious that a tune is independent of the metre, or of the lesser or greater numbers of syllables. . . . Rhymed poems, however, which are recited, and possess good metre, are neglected for something higher and more useful. . . ."

Al Khazari: "It is but proper that mere beauty of sound should yield to lucidity of speech. Harmony pleases the ear, but exactness makes the meaning clear. I see, however, that you Jews long for a prosody, in imitation of other peoples, in order to force the Hebrew language into their metres."

The Rabbi: "That is because we were and remain froward. Instead of being satisfied with our true superiority, we corrupted the structure of the language, which is built on harmony, and created discord. . . . . In matters of poetry we suffered what befell our forefathers, concerning whom it is written, They mingled among the Gentiles and learned their works". (Psalm cvi, 35).

Thus Jehudah Halevi considered rhyme and metre as foreign to the Hebrew language, and unnecessary to Hebrew poetry, which can exist in perfection quite independently of such ties. It may well be that modern Hebrew poetry will eventually find the inspiration of its Renaissance in the rejection of these bonds, and in the resumption of those earlier forms which offered fuller freedom to the Hebraic genius. And yet, with the inconsistency which may be allowed to great poets, Halevi uses both rhyme and metre with perfect and invariable success. His range was remarkable, though Heine somewhat exaggerates when he writes of him:

> *Der in heiligen Sirventen,*
> *Madrigalen und Terzinen,*
> *Kanzonetten und Ghaselen*
> *Ausgegossen alle Flammen.*

Perhaps, too, Heine's description of Jehudah Halevi as a *Minnesinger* is badly conceived. An essential feature of the *Minnesinger* was his wandering life, passing continually like Sir Walter Scott's Minstrel from court to court, from castle to castle. Worthy of close study as are Jehudah Halevi's love songs, wedding odes, elegies, epigrams, epistles, satires and riddles, yet it is not in these that he reached the summit of his genius. His noblest work is to be found in his religious and national meditations and songs. It is not always easy to distinguish between his so-called sacred and secular poems. Harkavy's division into secular and sacred is thus scarcely justified. A better distinction is Brody's, into liturgical and non-liturgical. For while some of Halevi's poems were intended for use in prayer and others were not so intended, the great mass of his work is impregnated with religious feeling. This is seen even in his love poems. These, often outspoken enough, are never coarse: a spiritual restraint is discernible amid the amatory abandonment. Often such a poem, in its opening words, indicates a human relationship; we read on and find that the lovers are God and Israel. It is as though to a lover that the poet sings:

> Would I might see his face within my heart!
> Mine eyes would never ask to look beyond.

The mystery and wonder of God and the Universe create a theme for many poems of great beauty, such as the one beginning:

> O Lord, where shall I find Thee?
>   All hidden and exalted is Thy place;
> And where shall I not find Thee?
>   Full of Thy glory is the infinite space.

And further:

>   Longing, I sought Thy presence;
> Lord, with my whole heart did I call and pray,
>   And going out toward Thee,
> I found Thee coming to me on the way,
>   Yea, in Thy wonders' might as clear to see
>   As when, within the shrine, I looked for Thee.

It is unnecessary to stress the point that Halevi's songs to Zion are his most beautiful works, displaying the deepest of his emotions. The greatest of these songs (No. 2 of this volume) is chanted to-day in Jewish congregations all over the world, on the Ninth of Ab, the fatal date on which, first by Babylon and again 656 years later by Rome, Jerusalem was laid waste. The ruling forces of the poet's life, the love and hope expressed in this Ode, have won him the sympathy and recognition of his posterity through the ages.

This great poet of the Jewish hope said of himself when singing to Zion of her further restoration, "I am a harp for thy songs." Here indeed we hear the real man. His love poems, as Ḥariẓi said, are made of dew and fire. But in his poems to Zion there is no such combination of a poet's ordinary artifices. It is his soul that is the instrument—and on his heartstrings is played the song of Israel's hope.

Many other compositions were modelled on Jehudah Halevi's Ode to Zion, as the liturgy for the Fast of Ab proves. These have their beauty, but the poets who followed Halevi appear to us like the stars after the moon has risen. In Spain the poets still sang because, for many years after Jehudah Halevi's death, his voice re-echoed in theirs. A poet and the begetter of poets—we need seek no more splendid epitaph for this "poet by the grace of God."

In the selection contained in the present volume it has been sought to present specimens of the poet's various styles and subjects. No selection can do Halevi justice. There are few poets who have maintained so consistently high a level; scarcely a line of his but deserves to be read.

The Hebrew text is, to a very large extent, that edited by Dr. Brody, and it is with great pleasure that I here record my sincere thanks for the privilege of using the results of his critical labours. The translation is in prose, with a tendency towards rhythm, and following the original, line by line; in some cases, however, there are added alternative translations in verse. As to the method of translating, only one remark need be offered. It has always seemed to the present translator at once unfair to a poet and displeasing to his readers to divest verses of their own peculiar dress. Thus in the Ode to Zion there seemed no reason for omitting Jehudah Halevi's reminiscence of Oholah and Oholibah, in order to soften down a somewhat harsh allusion. Nor, when rendering a love poem, does it seem just to turn Jehudah Halevi's own words:

> Would that, after my death, unto mine ears should come
> The sound of the golden bells upon thy skirts.

into:

> I think that I shall hear, when I am dead
> The rustle of thy gown, thy footsteps overhead.

To do these things may be attractive, but the oriental flavour is lost, and the poet is made to speak with the voice of a modern western writer, while clearly he was neither western nor modern.

I have to thank Dr. Israel Abrahams for constant encouragement, advice and unfailing support during the progress of this work. To Mr. Israel Zangwill likewise I owe a debt of gratitude for having read the proofs of the translation and for several useful suggestions; and also to Mr. Herbert Loewe for having given me much assistance in the proof-reading. And if I may permit myself to sound a further personal note for a moment, I should like to say this: I have loved Jehudah Halevi ever since, at my father's side, I began to read and understand his verses. If, by this volume, defective though it be in plan and imperfect in execution, I can win for Jehudah Halevi a new band of admirers, my own love for the poet will have borne its most precious fruit.

NINA SALAMAN

TEXT AND TRANSLATION

———

I. THE JOURNEY TO ZION

I

MY HEART IS IN THE EAST

My heart is in the east, and I in the utter-
    most west—
How can I find savour in food?   How shall it
    be sweet to me?
How shall I render my vows and my bonds,
    while yet
Zion lieth beneath the fetter of Edom, and I in
    Arab chains?
A light thing would it seem to me to leave all
    the good things of Spain—
Seeing how precious in mine eyes to behold the
    dust of the desolate sanctuary.

I

לבי במזרח

‏— ‏‎— | ‏‎— ‏‎— | ‏‎— ‏‎‏— ‏‎| ‏‎— ‏‎‏— ‏‎| ‏‎— ‏‎‏—‏

לִבִּי בְמִזְרָח וְאָנֹכִי בְּסוֹף מַעֲרָב
אֵיךְ אֶטְעֲמָה אֵת אֲשֶׁר־אֹכַל וְאֵיךְ יֶעֱרָב
אֵיכָה אֲשַׁלֵּם נְדָרַי וָאֱסָרַי בְּעוֹד
צִיּוֹן בְּחֶבֶל אֱדוֹם וַאֲנִי בְּכָבֶל עֲרָב
יֵקַל בְּעֵינַי עֲזֹב כָּל־טוּב סְפָרַד כְּמוֹ
יֵקַר בְּעֵינַי רְאוֹת עַפְרוֹת דְּבִיר נֶחֱרָב:

5

2

ODE TO ZION

(For rhymed version see page 151)

Zion! wilt thou not ask if peace be with thy
    captives
That seek thy peace—that are the remnant of
    thy flocks?

From west and east, from north and south—
    the greeting

I Kings 5,4. "Peace" from far and near, take thou from
    every side;

And greeting from the captive of desire,[1] giv-
    ing his tears like dew
Of Hermon, and longing to let them fall upon
    thine hills.

To wail for thine affliction I am like the jackals;
    but when I dream
Of the return of thy captivity, I am a harp for
    thy songs.

My heart to Bethel and Peniel yearneth sore,

Gen. 32, 2,3. To Maḥanaim and to all the places where thy
    pure ones have met.

There the Presence abideth in thee; yea, there
    thy Maker
Opened thy gates to face the gates of heaven.[2]

[1] Some editions have תקוה for תאוה.
[2] See No. 6, line 32.

2

צִיון הֲלֹא תִשְׁאֲלִי

‒ ‿ ‒ ‒ ‒ | ‿ ‒ ‒ | ‿ ‒ | ‿ ‒ ‒ ‒

צִיּוֹן הֲלֹא תִשְׁאֲלִי לִשְׁלוֹם אֲסִירָיִךְ
דּוֹרְשֵׁי שְׁלוֹמֵךְ וְהֵם יֶתֶר עֲדָרָיִךְ
מִיָּם וּמִזְרָח וּמִצָּפוֹן וְתֵימָן שְׁלוֹם
רָחוֹק וְקָרוֹב שְׂאִי מִכֹּל עֲבָרָיִךְ
וּשְׁלוֹם אֲסִיר תַּאֲוָה נוֹתֵן דְּמָעָיו כְּטַל־
חֶרְמוֹן וְנִכְסַף לְרִדְתָּם עַל הֲרָרָיִךְ   5
לִבְכּוֹת עֱנוּתֵךְ אֲנִי תַנִּים וְעֵת אֶחֱלֹם
שִׁיבַת שְׁבוּתֵךְ אֲנִי כִנּוֹר לְשִׁירָיִךְ
לִבִּי לְבֵית־אֵל וְלִפְנִיאֵל מְאֹד יֶהֱמֶה
וּלְמַחֲנַיִם וְכֹל פִּגְעֵי טְהוֹרָיִךְ   10
שָׁם הַשְּׁכִינָה שְׁכֵנָה לָךְ וְהַיֹּצְרֵךְ
פָּתַח לְמוּל שַׁעֲרֵי־שַׁחַק שְׁעָרָיִךְ

And the Lord's glory alone was thy light;
No sun nor moon nor stars were luminants for
   thee.

I would choose for my soul to pour itself out
   within that place
Where the spirit of God was outpoured upon
   thy chosen.

I Chron. 29,23. Thou art the house of royalty; thou art the
   throne of the Lord, and how[1]
Do slaves sit now upon thy princes' thrones?

Would I might be wandering in the places
   where
Gen. 35,7.   God was revealed unto thy seers and messen-
   gers.

Ps. 55,8.   O who will make me wings, that I may fly afar,
And lay the ruins of my cleft heart among thy
   broken cliffs!

I would fall, with my face upon thine earth and
   take delight
Ps. 102,15.   In thy stones and be tender to thy dust.

Neh. 2,3,5.   Yea, more, when standing by my fathers' tombs
Gen. 23,6.   I would marvel, in Hebron, over the chosen of
   thy graves.

I would pass into thy forest and thy fruitful
   field, and stand
Within thy Gilead, and wonder at thy mount
   beyond—[2]

[1] See Harkavy, who reads אִ'רְ, while Brody reads וְאִם.
[2] *i. e.* east of Jordan.

וּכְבוֹד אֲדֹנָי לְבַד הָיָה מְאוֹרֵךְ וְאֵין

שֶׁמֶשׁ וְסַהַר וְכוֹכָבִים מְאִירָיִךְ

אֶבְחַר לְנַפְשִׁי לְהִשְׁתַּפֵּךְ בְּמָקוֹם אֲשֶׁר   15

רוּחַ אֱלֹהִים שְׁפוּכָה עַל־בְּחִירָיִךְ

אַתְּ בֵּית מְלוּכָה וְאַתְּ כִּסֵּא אֲדֹנָי וְאִם

יָשְׁבוּ עֲבָדִים עֲלֵי כִסְאוֹת גְּבִירָיִךְ

מִי־יִתְּנֵנִי מְשׁוֹטֵט בַּמְּקוֹמוֹת אֲשֶׁר

נִגְלוּ אֱלֹהִים לְחֹזַיִךְ וְצִירָיִךְ   20

מִי יַעֲשֶׂה־לִּי כְנָפַיִם וְאַרְחִיק נְדֹד

אָנִיד לְבִתְרֵי לְבָבִי בֵּין בְּתָרָיִךְ

אֶפֹּל לְאַפִּי עֲלֵי אַרְצֵךְ וְאֶרְצֶה אֲבָ־

נַיִךְ מְאֹד וַאֲחֹנֵן אֶת־עֲפָרָיִךְ

אַף כִּי־בְעָמְדִי עֲלֵי קִבְרוֹת אֲבֹתַי וְאֶשְׁ־   25

תּוֹמֵם בְּחֶבְרוֹן עֲלֵי מִבְחַר קְבָרָיִךְ

אֶעְבֹר בְּיַעְרֵךְ וְכַרְמְלֵךְ וְאֶעֱמֹד בְּגִל־

עָדֵךְ וְאֶשְׁתּוֹמֲמָה אֶל־הַר עֲבָרָיִךְ

Deut. 32,49.50.   Mount Abarim, and Mount Hor, where are
the twain

Ps. 136,6.7.   Great lights—thy Luminaries, thy Teachers.

The life of souls is the air of thy land, and of
pure myrrh
The grains of thy dust, and honey from the
comb thy rivers.

Isa. 20,2.3   Sweet would it be unto my soul to walk naked
and barefoot
Upon the desolate ruins where thy holiest
dwellings were;

In the place of thine Ark where it is hidden[1]
and in the place
Of thy cherubim which abode in thine inner-
most recesses.

Jer. 7,29.   I will cut off and cast away the splendour of
my crown of locks, and curse the fate
That desecrated in unclean land the heads
that bore thy crown.

How shall it be sweet to me to eat and drink
while I behold

Jer. 15,3.   Dogs tearing at thy lions' whelps?

Eccles. 11,7.   Or how can light of day be joyous to mine
eyes while yet
I see in ravens' beaks torn bodies of thine
eagles?

O cup of sorrow! gently! hold a while! already

Ps. 38,8.   My loins are filled, yea, and my soul, with
thy bitterness.

[1] Yoma 52b–53b.

הַר הָעֲבָרִים וְהֹר הָהָר אֲשֶׁר־שָׁם שְׁנֵי

אוֹרִים גְּדֹלִים מְאִירַיִךְ וּמוֹרַיִךְ

חַיֵּי נְשָׁמוֹת אֲוִיר אַרְצֵךְ וּמִמָּר־דְּרוֹר

אַבְקַת עֲפָרֵךְ וְנֹפֶת צוּף נְהָרַיִךְ

יִנְעַם לְנַפְשִׁי הֲלֹךְ עָרֹם וְיָחֵף עֲלֵי

חָרְבוֹת שְׁמָמָה אֲשֶׁר הָיוּ דְּבִירָיִךְ

בִּמְקוֹם אֲרוֹנֵךְ אֲשֶׁר נִגְנַז וּבִמְקוֹם כְּרוּ־

בַיִךְ אֲשֶׁר שָׁכְנוּ חַדְרֵי חֲדָרָיִךְ

אָגֹז וְאַשְׁלִיךְ פְּאֵר נִזְרִי וְאָקֹב זְמָן

חִלַּל בְּאֶרֶץ טְמֵאָה אֶת־נְזִירָיִךְ

אֵיךְ יֶעֱרַב לִי אֲכֹל וּשְׁתוֹת בְּעֵת אֶחֱזֶה

כִּי יִסְחֲבוּ הַכְּלָבִים אֶת־כְּפִירָיִךְ

אוֹ אֵיךְ מְאוֹר יוֹם יְהִי מָתוֹק לְעֵינַי בְּעוֹד

אֶרְאֶה בְּפִי עֹרְבִים פִּגְרֵי נְשָׁרָיִךְ

כּוֹס הַיְגוֹנִים לְאַט הַרְפִּי מְעַט כִּי כְבָר

מָלְאוּ כְסָלַי וְנַפְשִׁי מִמְּרוֹרָיִךְ

When I remember Oholah I drink thy fury,

And I recall Oholibah, and drain thy dregs.

Zion! perfect in beauty! love and grace thou
     didst bind on to thee

Of olden time; and still the souls of thy com-
     panions are bound up with thee.

It is they that rejoice at thy well-being, that
     are in pain

Over thy desolation, and that weep over thy
     ruin—

They that, from the pit of the captive, pant
     toward thee, worshipping,

Every one from his own place, toward thy
     gates;

The flocks of thy multitude, which were ex-
     iled and scattered

From mount to hill, but have not forgotten
     thy fold;

Which grasp thy skirts and strengthen them-
     selves

To go up and take hold of the boughs of thy
     palms.

Shinar and Pathros[1]—were they equal unto
     thee in their greatness?

Can they compare their vanity[2] to thy
     Thummim and thy Urim?

And with whom could they compare thine
     anointed Kings?   and with whom

---

[1] Shinar refers to the moral and cultural achievements
of Bagdad, and Pathros to Byzantium, as representing
Mohammedan and Christian world-might.

[2] The reference here is to religious superstition.

Ezek. 23,4.
Isa. 51,17.
Ps. 75,9.
Lam. 2,15.

Zeph. 2,11.

Jer. 50,6.

I Sam. 15,27.
Cant. 7,9.

עֵת אֶזְכְּרָה אָהֳלָה אֲשַׁתָּה חֲמָתֵךְ וְאֶזְ־

כֹּר אָהֳלִיבָה וְאֶמְצָה אֶת־שְׁמָרֵיךְ 45

צִיּוֹן כְּלִילַת יֳפִי אַהֲבָה וְחֵן תִּקְשְׁרִי

מֵאָז וּבָךְ נִקְשְׁרוּ נַפְשׁוֹת חֲבֵרָיִךְ

הֵם הַשְּׂמֵחִים לְשַׁלְוָתֵךְ וְהַכֹּאֲבִים

עַל־שַׁמָּמוֹתֵךְ וּבֹכִים עַל־שִׁבְרָיִךְ 50

מִבּוֹר שְׁבִי שׁוֹאֲפִים נֶגְדֵּךְ וּמִשְׁתַּחֲוִים

אִישׁ מִמְּקוֹמוֹ אֱלֵי־נֹכַח שְׁעָרָיִךְ

עֶדְרֵי הֲמוֹנֵךְ אֲשֶׁר גָּלוּ וְהִתְפַּזְּרוּ

מֵהַר לְגִבְעָה וְלֹא שָׁכְחוּ גְדֵרָיִךְ

הַמַּחֲזִיקִים בְּשׁוּלַיִךְ וּמִתְאַמְּצִים 55

לַעֲלוֹת וְלֶאֱחֹז בְּסַנְסַנֵּי תְמָרָיִךְ

שִׁנְעָר וּפַתְרוֹס הֲיַעַרְכוּךְ בְּגָדְלָם וְאִם

הֶבְלָם יְדַמּוּ לְתֻמַּיִךְ וְאוּרָיִךְ

אֶל־מִי יְדַמּוּ מְשִׁיחַיִךְ וְאֶל־מִי נְבִי־

Thy prophets? and with whom thy minis-
    trants¹ and thy singers?

Isa. 2,18. He will change, He will wholly sweep away
    all the realms of idols;
Prov. 27,24. Thy splendour is for ever, from age to age
    thy crown.

Ps. 132,13. Thy God hath desired thee for a dwelling-
    place; and happy is the man
Ps. 65,5. Whom He chooseth and bringeth near that
    he may rest within thy courts.

Dan. 12,12. Happy is he that waiteth, that cometh nigh
    and seeth the rising
Of thy light, when on him thy dawn shall
    break—

Ps. 106,5. That he may see the welfare of thy chosen,
    and rejoice
Ezek. 16,55. In thy rejoicing, when thou turnest back unto
    thine olden youth.

¹ Those of the Levites who served and those who sang
in the Temple.

אֵיְךְ וְאֵל־מִי לְוָיֵךְ וְשָׂרָיֵךְ 60
יִשְׁנֶה וְיַחֲלֹף כְּלִיל כָּל־מַמְלְכוֹת הָאֱלִיל
חַסְנֵךְ לְעוֹלָם לְדוֹר וָדוֹר נְזָרֵיךְ
אַוֵּךְ לְמוֹשָׁב אֱלֹהַיִךְ וְאַשְׁרֵי אֱנוֹשׁ
יִבְחַר יְקָרֵב וְיִשְׁכֹּן בַּחֲצֵרָיֵךְ
אַשְׁרֵי מְחַכֶּה וְיַגִּיעַ וְיִרְאֶה עֲלוֹת 65
אוֹרֵךְ וְיִבָּקְעוּ עָלָיו שְׁחָרָיֵךְ
לִרְאוֹת בְּטוֹבַת בְּחִירַיֵךְ וְלַעֲלֹז בְּשִׂמְ־
חָתֵךְ בְּשׁוּבֵךְ אֱלֵי קַדְמַת נְעוּרָיֵךְ:

3

TO MOUNT ABARIM

Peace be to thee, Mount Abarim!

I Kings 5,4 Peace be to thee on every side![1]

Within thee is gathered the chosen of mankind,

Gen. 23,6. In thee is the chosen of all sepulchres.

If thou knowest him not, ask thou

Ps. 136,13. Of the Red Sea which was rent apart;

And ask of the bush and ask of the mount—

Jud. 5,29. Ask of Sinai—they shall return answer unto
　　　　thee:

Num. 12,7.
Haggai 1,13. He that faithfully bore the message of God,

Exodus 4,10. Even though no man of words!

Ps. 54,6. God helping,

I have vowed an early pilgrimage to thee.

---

[1] Play of words on עברים.

3

הר העברים

‐ ‐ | ‐ ⏑ ‐ | ‐ ⏑ ‐ :

שָׁלוֹם לְךָ הַר הָעֲבָרִים

שָׁלוֹם לְךָ מִכָּל־עֲבָרִים

בָּךְ נֶאֱסַף מִבְחַר אֱנוֹשׁ

וַיְהִי בְךָ מִבְחַר קְבָרִים

אִם־לֹא יְדַעְתָּהוּ שְׁאַל   5

יַם־סוּף אֲשֶׁר נִגְזַר גְּזָרִים

וּשְׁאַל סְנֶה וּשְׁאַל לְהַר

סִינַי יְשִׁיבוּךָ אֲמָרִים

הַנֶּאֱמָן עַל־מַלְאֲכוּת

הָאֵל וְהוּא לֹא אִישׁ דְּבָרִים   10

אִם הָאֱלֹהִים עֶזְרִי

עָלַי לְשַׁחֲרָךְ נְדָרִים׃

4

MY DREAM

<table>
<tr><td>Ps. 84.2.</td><td>My God, Thy dwelling-places are lovely!</td></tr>
<tr><td>Num. 12.8.</td><td>It is in vision and not in dark speeches that
    Thou art near.</td></tr>
</table>

<table>
<tr><td>Ps. 73.17.</td><td>My dream did bring me into the sanctuaries
    of God,
And I beheld His beautiful services;</td></tr>
<tr><td>Num. 29.16.</td><td>And the burnt-offering and meal-offering and
    drink-offering,
And round about, heavy clouds of smoke.
And it was ecstasy to me to hear the Levites'
    song,
In their council for the order of services.</td></tr>
</table>

<table>
<tr><td>Ps. 139.18.</td><td>I awoke, and I was yet with Thee, O God,
And I gave thanks, and it was sweet to thank
    Thee.</td></tr>
</table>

4

חלומי

‌ ‌ ‌ ‌ ᵕ – – | – ᵕ – | – – – | ᵕ – ᵕ |

אֱלֹהַי מִשְׁכְּנוֹתֶיךָ יְדִידוֹת

וְקֵרַבְתָּ בְּמַרְאֶה לֹא בְחִידוֹת

הֲבִיאַנִי חֲלוֹמִי מִקְדְּשֵׁי אֵל

וְשֵׁרַתִּי מַלְאֲכוֹתָיו הַחֲמֻדוֹת

וְהָעוֹלָה וּמִנְחָתָה וְנִסְכָּה

וְסָבִיב תִּימֲרוֹת עָשָׁן כְּבֵדוֹת 5

וְנֶעֱמָתִּי בְּשָׁמְעִי שִׁיר לְוִיִּם

בְּסוֹדֵיהֶם לְסֵדֶר הָעֲבֹדוֹת

הֲקִיצוֹתִי וְעוֹדִי עִמְּךָ אֵל

וְהוֹדֵיתִי וְלָךְ נָאֶה לְהוֹדוֹת: 10

5

EQUIPPED FOR FLIGHT

Wilt thou yet pursue youth after twoscore
    years and ten
Since thy days are equipped for flight?
And wilt thou flee from the service of God
And long for the service of men?
And wilt thou seek the face of many

Ps. 111,2.   And forsake the face of One sought out for
    all delight?

Jos. 9,12.   And art thou too slothful to take provision
    for thy way,

And wilt thou sell thy portion for a mess of
    pottage?

Prov. 30,15-16. Saith not thy soul yet unto thee, 'Enough',

Ezek. 47,12. But reneweth her desire month by month?

Incline from her counsel to the counsel of God,
And turn aside from the five senses;
And make thyself acceptable to thy Creator
    for the rest
Of thy days which press on and hasten;

Ps. 12,3.   And seek not with a double heart for His
    favour

Num. 24,1. And go not to meet good omens,

5

לְהִתְעוֹפֵף חֲמִשִּׁים

‒ ‒ ‒ ◡ ‒ | ‒ ‒ | ‒ ‒ ◡ ‒ ‖

הֲתִרְדֹּף נַעֲרוּת אַחַר חֲמִשִּׁים
וְיָמֶיךָ לְהִתְעוֹפֵף חֲמָשִׁים

וְתִבְרַח מֵעֲבֹדַת הָאֱלֹהִים
וְתִכְסֹף אֶל־עֲבֹדַת הָאֲנָשִׁים

וְתִדְרֹשׁ אֶת־פְּנֵי רַבִּים וְתִטֹּשׁ   5
פְּנֵי אֶחָד לְכָל־חֵפֶץ דְּרוּשִׁים

וְתֵעָצֵל לְהִצְטַיֵּד לְדַרְכָּךְ
וְתִמְכֹּר חֶלְקְךָ בִּנְזִיד עֲדָשִׁים

הֲלֹא אָמְרָה־לְּךָ עוֹד נַפְשְׁךָ הוֹן
וְתַאֲוָתָהּ תְּבַכֵּר לַחֲדָשִׁים   10

נְטֵה מֵעַל עֲצָתָהּ אֶל־עֲצַת־אֵל
וְסוּר מֵעַל חֲמֵשֶׁת הָרְגָשִׁים

וְהִתְרַצֵּה לְיֹצֶרְךָ בְּיֶתֶר
יְמוֹתֶיךָ אֲשֶׁר אָצִים וְחָשִׁים

וְאַל־תִּדְרֹשׁ בְּלֵב וָלֵב רְצוֹנוֹ   15
וְאַל־תֵּלֵךְ לְךָ לִקְרַאת נְחָשִׁים

But to do His will be strong as a leopard,
Swift as a roe, and mighty as a lion.

Ps. 46,3. And let not thine heart be shaken in the heart
of the seas,

Isa. 54,10. When thou beholdest mountains move and
totter,

Jer. 38,12. And seamen with hands limp as rags,[1]
And wise craftsmen standing dumb,[2]
Which joyfully went face forward,
But turn their backs ashamed;
And only the ocean before thee for a haven,
And no refuge for thee, but snares,
And the sails quiver and shake,
And the beams stagger and strain,
And the hand of the wind playeth with the
waters
Like men lifting sheaves in the threshing;
And now it maketh of them threshing-floors,
And anon it maketh of them stacks of sheaves.
When they prevail they come like lions,
And when they faint they creep like snakes,
The last chasing the first,

Jer. 8,17. Like adders which will not be charmed,
Ex. 15,10. And the mighty ship falleth like an atom by
Isa. 33,21.   the blow of a mighty one,
Isa. 10,34.
Ezek. 16,47.

---

[1] Play on words, מַלָּחִים (seamen) מְלָחִים (rags).

[2] See play on words in the Hebrew text.

הָיָה לַעֲשׂוֹת רְצוֹנוֹ עַז כְּנָמֵר
וְקַל כִּצְבִי וְגִבּוֹר כַּלְּיָשִׁים
וְאַל־יִמּוֹט בְּלֵב יַמִּים לְבָבֶךָ
וְהָרִים תֶּחֱזֶה מָטִים וּמָשִׁים　　　　　20
וּמַלָּחִים יְדֵיהֶם כַּמְּלָחִים
וְחַכְמֵי הַחֲרָשִׁים מַחֲרִישִׁים
שְׂמֵחִים הֹלְכִים נֹכַח פְּנֵיהֶם
וְשָׁבִים אֶל־אַחֲרֵיהֶם וּבֹשִׁים
וְאָקְיָנוֹס לְפָנֶיךָ לְמָנוֹס　　　　　25
וְאֵין מִבְרָח לְךָ כִּי אִם־יְקוּשִׁים
וְיָמוּטוּ וְיָנוּטוּ קְלָעִים
וְיָנוּעוּ וְיָזוּעוּ קְרָשִׁים
וְיַד־רוּחַ מְצַחֶקֶת בְּמַיִם
כְּנֹשְׂאֵי הָעֳמָרִים בַּדִּישִׁים　　　　　30
וּפַעַם תַּעֲשֶׂה מֵהֶם גְּרָנוֹת
וּפַעַם תַּעֲשֶׂה מֵהֶם גְּדִישִׁים
בְּעֵת הִתְגַּבְּרָם דָּמוּ אֲרָיוֹת
וְעֵת הֶחָלְשָׁם דָּמוּ נְחָשִׁים
וְרִאשֹׁנִים דְּלָקוּם אַחֲרֹנִים　　　　　35
כְּצִפְעֹנִים וְאֵין לָהֶם לְחָשִׁים
וְצִי אַדִּיר כְּקָט יִפֹּל בְּאַדִּיר

Isa. 33,23.	And the mast and the sails are grown weak,
	And the ark and her chambers are confused,
Gen. 6,14–16.	The lowest with the second and the third;
	And they that pull the ropes are in travail,[1]
	And women and men in desperation,[1]
Isa. 33,23.	And the spirit is gone from their pilots,
	And the bodies are weary of the souls,
Gen. 36,26.	There is no worth in the strength of the masts,
	And no desire for the guidance of the old men;
Job 41,21.	And the cedar-masts are accounted as stubble,
	The fir beams as if they were reeds.
Prov. 27,3.	And the ballast of sand on the surface of the
	sea is like a straw,
Isa. 5,24.	And the iron sockets are like bits of chaff,
	And the people pray, each one to his holy one,
	But thou turnest to the Holy of Holies,
	And rememberest the marvels of the Red Sea
	and the Jordan,
Jer. 17,1.	Which are graven upon all hearts.
Ps. 65,8.	Thou praisest Him that stilleth the roaring
	of the seas,
Isa. 57,20.	When its waters cast up mire;
	And while thou recallest unto Him the abom-
	inations[2] of unclean hearts
	He recalleth for thee the merit of the saintly
	fathers.

[1] See play on words in Hebrew text.

[2] Following Harkavy's opinion that זָנוּת should be read in place of זְכוֹת.

וְהַתֹּרֶן וְהַנֵּס נֶחֱלָשִׁים

וְהַתֵּבָה וְקִנְיָנֶיהָ נִבְכִּים

כְּתַחְתִּים שְׁנַיִם כַּשְּׁלִשִׁים 40

וּמֹשְׁכֵי הַחֲבָלִים בַּחֲבָלִים

וְנָשִׁים וַאֲנָשִׁים נֶאֱנָשִׁים

וְרוּחַ חֻבְּלָה מֵחֹבְלֵיהֶם

וְקָצוּ הַגְּוִיּוֹת בַּנְּפָשִׁים

וְאֵין יִתְרוֹן לְחֹזֶק הַתְּרָנִים 45

וְאֵין חֶמְדָּה לְתַחְבֻּלַת יְשִׁישִׁים

וְנֶחְשְׁבוּ לְקַשׁ תָּרְנֵי אֲרָזִים

וְנֶהֶפְכוּ לְקָנִים הַבְּרוֹשִׁים

וְנֶטַּל חוֹל בְּגַב הַיָּם כְּתָבָן

וּבַרְזִלֵּי אֲדָנִים כַּחֲשָׁשִׁים 50

וְעָם יִתְפַּלְּלוּ כָל־אִישׁ לְקָדְשׁוֹ

וְאַתְּ פְּנֵה לְקֹדֶשׁ הַקֳּדָשִׁים

וְתִזְכֹּר מִפְלְאוֹת יַם־סוּף וְיַרְדֵּן

אֲשֶׁר עַל־כָּל־לְבָבוֹת הֵם חֲרוּשִׁים

תְּשַׁבַּח לַמַּשְׁבִּיחַ שְׁאוֹן יָם 55

בְּעֵת שֶׁיִּגְרְשׁוּ מֵימָיו רְפָשִׁים

וְתִזְכָּר־לוֹ זְנוּת לִבּוֹת טְמֵאִים

וְיִזְכָּר־לָךְ זְכוּת אָבוֹת קְדֹשִׁים

He will renew His wondrous deeds when thou
    renewest
Before Him the dancing song of Maḥli and
    Mushi's sons;[1]
And He will restore the souls to the bodies,
And the dry bones shall come to life.

Ps.107,29-30.   Then in a moment the waves are stilled,
I Sam. 30,16.   Like flocks spread abroad upon the field;
And the night, when the sun hath come down
    the steps
Of the starry host, captained now by the moon,
Ps. 45,14   Is like an Ethiopian woman in raiment of gold
Ex. 39,13.   And of blue inset with crystals.
And the stars are confused in the heart of the
    sea
Like strangers driven out of their homes;
And after their image, in their likeness,
    they make light
In the sea's heart, like flames of fire.
The face of the waters and the face of the
    heavens, the infinity of sea,
The infinity of night, are grown pure, are
    made clear,
And the sea appeareth as a firmament—[2]
Then are they two seas bound up together;
And between them is my heart, a third sea,
Ps. 89,10.   Lifting up ever anew my waves of praise.

---

[1] Names of tribes of Levitic singers in the Temple.
[2] בעינו might mean either "in its essence"—in other
words that the sky and the sea look exactly alike, or—that
the firmament is reflected in the sea. In any case this
line is leading up to the idea of the next three lines.

יְחַדֵּשׁ נוֹרְאוֹתָיו כִּי תְחַדֵּשׁ

לְפָנָיו שִׁיר מָחוֹל מַחְלִים וּמוּשִׁים 60

וְיָשִׁיב הַנְּשָׁמוֹת לַפְּגָרִים

וְיִחְיוּ הָעֲצָמִים הַיְבֵשִׁים

וְרֶגַע יִשְׁתְּקוּ גַלִּים וְיִדְמוּ

עֲדָרִים עַל־פְּנֵי אֶרֶץ נְטָשִׁים

וְהַלַּיְל כָּבוֹא שֶׁמֶשׁ בְּמַעֲלוֹת 65

צְבָא מָרוֹם וְעָלָיו שַׂר חֲמִשִּׁים

כְּכוּשִׁית מִשְׁבְּצוֹת זָהָב לְבוּשָׁה

וְכִתְכֵלֶת בְּמִלֵּאת גְּבִישִׁים

וְכוֹכָבִים בְּלֵב הַיָּם נְבֻכִים

כְּגֵרִים מִמְּעוֹנֵיהֶם גְּרוּשִׁים 70

וְכִדְמוּתָם בְּצַלְמָם יַעֲשׂוּ אוֹר

בְּלֵב הַיָּם כְּלֶהָבוֹת וְאִשִּׁים

פְּנֵי מַיִם וְשָׁמַיִם עֲדִי־יָם

עֲדֵי לַיְל מְטֹהָרִים לְטוּשִׁים

וְיָם דּוֹמֶה לָרָקִיעַ בְּעֵינוּ 75

שְׁנֵיהֶם אָז שְׁנֵי יַמִּים חֲבוּשִׁים

וּבֵינוֹתָם לְבָבִי יָם שְׁלִישִׁי

בְּשׂוֹא גַלֵּי שְׁבָחַי הַחֲדָשִׁים:

6

FOR THE SAKE OF THE HOUSE OF OUR GOD

The singer's reply to one who reproved him for his long-
ing to go to the Land of Israel

Cant. 5,5.   Thy words are compounded of sweet-smelling
        myrrh
    And gathered from the rock of the mountains
        of spice,
    And unto thee and the house of thy fathers
        belong precious virtues
    Whereunto praises fail to attain.
    Thou comest to meet me with sweet speeches,
    But within them lie men in wait bearing
        swords—
    Words wherein stinging bees lurk,[1]

Is. 33,12.   A honeycomb prickly with thorns.
    If the peace of Jerusalem is not to be sought

II Sam. 5,6.8.   While yet with the blind and the halt she
        is filled,

Ps. 122,8–9.   For the sake of the House of our God let us
        seek
    Her peace, or for the sake of friends and of
        brothers;

Gen. 44,10.   And if it be according to your words, see, there
Jos. 2,21.   is sin
    Upon all those who bend towards her and bow
        down,
    And sin upon those sires who dwelt in her
        as strangers,
    And purchased there vaults for their dead.

[1] Note the play on the words דְּבָרִים and דְּבֹרִים.

6

למען בית אלהינו

תשובת המשורר לאדם שכתב לו תוכחה על תשוקתו ללכת לארץ ישראל

‖ — ‿ | — — ‿ | — — ‿ | — — ‿

דְּבָרֶיךָ בְּמוֹר עֹבֵר רְקֻחִים
וּמִצּוּר הַרֲרֵי הַמּוֹר לְקֻחִים

וְלָךְ וּלְבֵית אֲבֹתֶיךָ חֲמָדוֹת
אֲשֶׁר יִלְאוּ לְהַשִּׂיגָם שְׁבָחִים

פְּגַשְׁתַּנִי בְּמִדְבָּרִים עֲרֵבִים   5
בְּתוֹכָם אֹרְבִים נֹשְׂאֵי שְׁלָחִים

דְּבָרִים אֹרְבוּ תוֹכָם דְּבָרִים
וְתוֹךְ יַעֲרַת דְּבַשׁ קוֹצִים כְּסוּחִים

וְאִם כִּי־לֹא שְׁלוֹם שָׁלֵם יְבַקֵּשׁ
בְּעוֹדָהּ מְלֵאָה עִוְרִים וּפִסְחִים   10

לְמַעַן בֵּית אֱלֹהֵינוּ נְבַקֵּשׁ
שְׁלוֹמָהּ אוֹ בְּעַד רֵעִים וְאַחִים

וְאִם כֵּן־דְּהוּא כְּדִבְרֵיכֶם רְאוּ חַטָא
עֲלֵי כָל־קָרֲעִים נֶגְדָּהּ וְשֹׁחִים

וְחַטָא הוֹרִים שְׁכָנוּהָ כְּגֵרִים   15
וְקָנוּ שָׁם לְמֵתֵיהֶם צְרִיחִים

And vain would be the deed of the fathers who
     were embalmed
And their bodies sent to her earth—
And they sighing for her sake
Though the land was full of reprobates;
And for naught would the fathers' altars have
     been built,
And in vain their oblation offered there.

Is it well that the dead should be remembered,
And the Ark and the Tablets forgotten?
That we should seek out the place of the pit
     and the worm,
And forsake the fount of life eternal?
Have we any heritage save the sanctuaries of
     God?—
Then how should we forget His holy Mount?
Have we either in the east or in the west
A place of hope wherein we may trust,
Except the land that is full of gates,
Toward which the gates of Heaven are open—
Like Mount Sinai and Carmel and Bethel,
And the houses of the prophets, the envoys,
And the thrones of the priests of the Lord's
     throne,
And the thrones of the kings, the anointed?
Unto us, yea, and unto our children, hath
     He assigned her;

וְתֹהוּ מַעֲשֵׂה אָבוֹת חֲנֻטִים

וּפִגְרֵיהֶם אֱלֵי אַרְצָה שְׁלוּחִים

וְהָיוּ בַעֲבוּרָה נֶאֱנָחִים

וְהָאָרֶץ מְלֵאָה נֶאֱלָחִים 20

וְלָרִיק מִזְבְּחוֹת אָבוֹת בְּנוּיִים

וְלַשָּׁוְא קֵרְבוּ שָׁם הַזְּבָחִים

הֲטוֹב שֶׁיִּהְיוּ מֵתִים זְכוּרִים

וְהָאָרוֹן וְהַלֻּחוֹת שְׁכוּחִים

נְשַׁחֵר אֶת־מְקוֹם שַׁחַת וְרִמָּה 25

וְנִטֹּשׁ אֶת־מְקוֹר חַיֵּי נְצָחִים

הֲלָנוּ נַחֲלָה רַק מִקְדְּשֵׁי־אֵל

וְאֵיךְ נִהְיֶה לְהַר קָדְשׁוֹ שְׁכֵחִים

הֲיֵשׁ לָנוּ בְמִזְרָח אוֹ בְּמַעְרָב

מְקוֹם תִּקְוָה נְהִי עָלָיו בְּטוּחִים 30

אֲבָל אֶרֶץ אֲשֶׁר מָלְאָה שְׁעָרִים

לְנֶגְדָּם שַׁעֲרֵי־שַׁחַק פְּתוּחִים

כְּהַר סִינַי וְהַכַּרְמֶל וּבֵית־אֵל

וּבָתֵּי הַנְּבִיאִים הַשְּׁלוּחִים

וְכִסְאוֹת כֹּהֲנֵי כִסֵּא אֲדֹנָי 35

וְכִסְאוֹת הַמְּלָכִים הַמְּשָׁחִים

וְלָנוּ גַּם־לְבָנֵינוּ יְעָדָהּ

Isa. 13,21.   And though wild beasts abide in her, and dole-
　　　　　　　　ful creatures,
　　　　　　　Was it not so she was given of old to the
　　　　　　　　fathers—
　　　　　　　All of her the heritage of thorns and thistles?

Gen. 13,17.   But they walked through the length and the
　　　　　　　　breadth of her
　　　　　　　As one walketh in an orchard among the
　　　　　　　　green boughs,

I Chron.29,15. Though they came as strangers and sojourn-
　　　　　　　　ers, seeking

Gen. 23,4.   But burial place and a lodging there, like way-
　　　　　　　　farers.
　　　　　　　And there they walked before the Lord
　　　　　　　And learnt the straight paths.
　　　　　　　And they said that here arise the shades
　　　　　　　And those who lie under the bars of earth
　　　　　　　　come forth,
　　　　　　　And that here the bodies rejoice,
　　　　　　　And the souls return to their rest.

　　　　　　　See now, yea see, my friend, and understand

Prov. 22,5.   And turn aside from the lure of thorns and
　　　　　　　　snares,
　　　　　　　And let not the wisdom of the Greeks beguile
　　　　　　　　thee,
　　　　　　　Which hath no fruit, but only flowers—
　　　　　　　Or her fruit is, that the earth was never out-
　　　　　　　　stretched

Isa. 40,22.   Nor the tents of the sky spread out,
　　　　　　　Nor was any beginning to all the work of creation
　　　　　　　Nor will any end be to the renewal of the
　　　　　　　　months.[1]

　　　　　　　[1] A reference to the doctrine of the eternity of matter.

וְאִם צִיִּים שְׁכָנוּהָ וְאֹחִים

הֲלֹא כֵן נִתְּנָה קֶדֶם לְאָבוֹת

וְכָלָה נַחֲלַת קוֹצִים וְחֹחִים 40

וְהֵם מִתְהַלְּכִים אָרְכָּהּ וְרָחְבָּהּ

כְּמִתְהַלֵּךְ בְּפַרְדֵּס בֵּין צְמָחִים

וְהֵם גֵּרִים וְתוֹשָׁבִים וְדֹרְשִׁים

מְקוֹם־קֶבֶר וּמָלוֹן שָׁם כְּאֹרְחִים

וְשָׁם הִתְהַלְּכוּ לִפְנֵי אֲדֹנָי 45

וְלָמְדוּ הַשְּׁבִילִים הַנְּכֹחִים

וְאָמְרוּ כִּי־רְפָאִים שָׁם יְקוּמוּן

וְיֵצְאוּ שֹׁכְבִים תַּחַת בְּרִיחִים

וְכִי שָׁם תַּעֲלֶינָה הַגְּוִיּוֹת

וְתָשֹׁבְנָה נְפָשׁוֹת לַמְּנוּחִים 50

רְאֵה נָא גַּם־דְּאֵה דּוֹדִי וְהָבֵן

וְסוּר מִמְּוֹקְשִׁים צִנִּים וּפַחִים

וְאַל־תַּשִּׂיאֲךָ חָכְמַת יְוָנִית

אֲשֶׁר אֵין־לָהּ פְּרִי כִּי אִם־פְּרָחִים

וּפִרְיָהּ כִּי אֲדָמָה לֹא רְקוּעָה 55

וְכִי לֹא אָהֳלֵי־שַׁחַק מְתוּחִים

וְאֵין רֵאשִׁית לְכָל־מַעֲשֵׂה בְרֵאשִׁית

וְאֵין אַחֲרִית לְחִדּוּשׁ הַיְרָחִים

Hark how the words of her wise are confused,
Built and plastered up on a vain unstable base;
Neh. 5.13. And thou wilt come back with a heart stripped
     empty
I Kings 18.27. And a mouth full of dross and weeds.

Jud. 5,6. Wherefore, then, should I seek me out crooked
     ways,
And forsake the mother of paths?

שְׁמַע דִּבְרֵי נְבוֹנֶיהָ נְבֻכִים
בְּנוּיִים עַל־יְסוֹד תֹּהוּ וְטִיחִים
וְתָשׁוּב לָךְ בְּלֵב רֵיקָם וְנָעוּר
וּפֶה מָלֵא בְּרֹב שִׁינִים וְשִׂיחִים.
וְלָמָּה־זֶּה אֲבַקֶּשׁ־לִי אֳרָחוֹת
עֲקַלְקַלּוֹת וְאֶעֱזֹב אֹם אֳרָחִים:

7

WHEN MY SOUL LONGED

The Beginning of His Journey

Ps. 84,3. That day when my soul longed for the place
  of assembly,
Yet a dread of departure seized hold of me,
He, great in counsel, prepared for me ways
  for setting forth,
And I found His name in my heart a sustain-
  ment.
Therefore I bow down to Him at every stage;
And at every step I thank Him.

7

יום נכספה נפשי
בתחלת מסעיו לארץ ישראל

‐ ‐ ‐ ⌣ ‐ | ‐ ‐ ‐ | ‐ ‐ ⌣ ‐ | ‐ ‐ ‐ ▪

יוֹם נִכְסְפָה נַפְשִׁי לְבֵית הַוָּעֵד

וַיֹּאחֲזֵנִי לַנְּדֻדִים רָעַד

סִבֵּב גְּדָל־יֵעֵצָה עֲלִילוֹת לַנְּדֹד

וָאָמְצָאָה לִשְׁמוֹ בְּלִבִּי סָעַד

עַל־כֵּן אֲנִי מִשְׁתַּחֲוֶה אֵלָיו בְּכָל־

מַסָּע וְאֹדֶנּוּ עֲלֵי כָל־צָעַד:

5

8

BEAUTIFUL OF ELEVATION
(For rhymed version see page 157)

Ps. 48.3.	Beautiful of elevation! Joy of the world! City of the Great King!
Ps. 84.3.	For thee my soul is longing from limits of the west.
Isa. 63.15.	The tumult of my tenderness is stirred when I remember Thy glory of old that is departed—thine habitation which is desolate.
Ex. 19.4.	O that I might fly on eagles' wings, That I might water thy dust with my tears until they mingle together.
Jer. 8.19.	I have sought thee, even though thy King be not in thee and though, in place
Deut. 8.15.	Of thy Gilead's balm, are now the fiery serpent and the scorpion.
Ps. 102.15.	Shall I not be tender to thy stones and kiss them, And the taste of thy soil be sweeter than honey unto me?

8

יפה נוף משוש תבל

‒ ‒ ‒ ◡ ‒ | ‒ ‒ ‒ ◡ ‒

קִרְיָה לְמֶלֶךְ רָב	יְפֵה נוֹף מְשׂוֹשׂ תֵּבֵל
מִפְּאֲתֵי מַעְרָב	לָךְ נִכְסְפָה נַפְשִׁי
כִּי אֶזְכְּרָה קֶדֶם	הֲמוֹן רַחֲמַי נִכְמָר
וְנָוֵךְ אֲשֶׁר חָרֵב	כְּבוֹדַךְ אֲשֶׁר גָּלָה
כַּנְפֵי נְשָׁרִים עַד	וּמִי־יִתְּנֵנִי עַל־
עֲפָרֵךְ וְיִתְעָרֵב	אֲרַוֶּה בְדִמְעָתִי
אֵין בָּךְ וְאִם בִּמְקוֹם	דְּרַשְׁתִּיךְ וְאִם מַלְכֵּךְ
שָׂרָף וְגַם עַקְרָב	צֳרִי גִלְעָדֵךְ נָחָשׁ
אֲחֹנֵן וְאֶשָּׁקֵם	הֲלֹא אֶת־אֲבָנַיִךְ
לְפִי מִדְבַּשׁ יָעֱרָב:	וְטַעַם רְגָבַיִךְ

9

ON THE SEA.

I

My God, break not the breakers of the sea,
Nor say Thou to the deep, 'Be dry',
Until I thank Thy mercies, and I thank
The waves of the sea and the wind of the west;
Let them waft me to the place of the yoke of
    Thy love,
And bear far from me the Arab yoke.
And how shall my desires not find fulfilment,
Seeing I trust in Thee, and Thou art pledged
    to me?[1]

Isa. 44,27.

[1] See play on words in the Hebrew rhymes of lines 6 and 8.

9

מִשְׁבְּרֵי־יָם

I

‏– – – | – – ‿ – | – – ‿ – | – – ‿

אֱלֹהַי אַל תְּשַׁבֵּר מִשְׁבְּרֵי־יָם
וְאַל־תֹּאמַר לְצוּלַת יָם חֲרָבִי
עֲדֵי אוֹדֶה חֲסָדֶיךָ וְאוֹדָה
לְגַלֵּי יָם וְרוּחַ מַעֲרָבִי
יְקָרְבוּ מְקוֹם עַל אַהֲבָתָךְ
וּמֵעָלַי יְסִירוּן עַל עֲרָבִי
וְאֵיךְ לֹא־יִתַּמּוּ לִי מִשְׁאֲלוֹתַי
וּבְךָ אֶבְטַח וְאַתָּה הוּא עֲרָבִי:

10

ON THE SEA.

II

Hath the flood come again and made the
    world a waste
So that one cannot see the face of the dry
    land,
And no man is there and no beast and no
    bird?
Isa. 50,11.   Have they all come to an end and lain down
    in sorrow?[1]
To see even mountain or marsh would be a
    rest for me,
And the desert itself would be sweet.
But I look on every side and there is nothing
But only water and sky and ark,
Job 41,23–24.   And Leviathan making the abyss to boil,
So that one deemeth the deep to be hoary.
And the heart of the sea concealeth the ship
As though she were a stolen thing in the sea's
    hand.
And the sea rageth and my soul exulteth—
For to the sanctuary of her God she draweth
    near.

---

[1] The text has ושכנו מעצבה, but reference to Isa. 50,11
will show that it should read ושכבו.

10

מִשְׁבְּרֵי יָם

II

‒ ‒ | ‒ | ‒ ‒ ‒ | ‒ ‒ ‿ | ‒ ‒ ‒ | ‒

הֲבָא מַבּוּל וְשָׁם תֵּבֵל חֲרֵבָה

וְאֵין לִרְאוֹת פְּנֵי אֶרֶץ חֲרֵבָה

וְאֵין אָדָם וְאֵין חַיָּה וְאֵין עוֹף

הֲסָף הַכֹּל וְשָׁכְנוּ מַעֲצֵבָה

וּבִרְאוֹת הַר וְשׁוּחָה לִי מְנוּחָה   5

וְאֶרֶץ הָעֲרָבָה לִי עֲרֵבָה

וְאַשְׁגִּיחַ לְכָל־עֵבֶר וְאֵין־כֹּל

אֲבָל מַיִם וְשָׁמַיִם וְתֵבָה

וְלִוְיָתָן בְּהַרְתִּיחוֹ מְצוּלָה   10

וְאֶחְשֹׁב כִּי תְהוֹם יַחְשֹׁב לְשֵׂיבָה

וְלֵב הַיָּם יְכַחֵשׁ בָּאֳנִיָּה

כְּאִלּוּ הִיא בְּיַד־הַיָּם גְּנֵבָה

וְיָם יִזְעַף וְנַפְשִׁי תַעֲלֹז כִּי

אֱלֵי מִקְדַּשׁ אֱלֹהֶיהָ קְרֵבָה:

II

ON THE SEA.

III

To Thee my soul turneth in trust or fear,
'Tis to Thee she giveth ever thanks and
    worship;
In Thee I rejoice on the day I wander forth
    and flee,
And Thee I thank in every flight and wander-
    ing—
Yea, when the ship, to bear me over, spreadeth
    out
Wings like the wings of a stork,
And when the deep groaneth and roareth
    beneath me,
As though it had learnt from mine own
    entrails,
Job 41,23.   And maketh the abyss to seethe like a pot,
Yea, turneth the sea into a pot of burning
    ointment;
Num. 24,24. And when the ship from Kittim cometh to
    the sea of the Philistines
II Kings 6,9. And the Hittites come down to the stronghold;
And when creatures press upon the ship
And sea-monsters watch for food,
Jer. 4,31.   And there is a time of trouble as of one that
    bringeth forth her first child, when children

‖

משברי ים

III

_ _ _ | ‿ _ _ _ | _ _ _ | _ ‿ _

לָךְ נַפְשִׁי בְּטוּחָה אוֹ חֲרֵדָה

לָךְ מִשְׁתַּחֲוָה תָּמִיד וּמוֹדָה

בָּךְ אֶשְׂמַח בְּיוֹם אָנַע וְאָנוּד

וְלָךְ אוֹדֶה בְּכָל־נִיעָה וְנִידָה

וּבְפָרֹשׂ הַסְּפִינָה לַעֲבָר בִּי   5

כְּנָפַיִם כְּכַנְפֵי הַחֲסִידָה

וְעֵת תָּהֹם תְּהוֹם תַּחְתַּי וְתֶנְהַם

כְּאִלּוּ מִקְּרָבַי הִיא לָמֵדָה

וְתַרְתִּיחַ כְּסִיר אֶת־הַמְּצוּלָה

וְיָם תָּשִׂים כְּמֶרְקָחָה יְקוּדָה   10

וְצִים כִּתִּים בְּבוֹאָם יָם פְּלִשְׁתִּים

וְהַחְתִּים נֶחְתִּים בַּמְּצוּדָה

וְהַחַיּוֹת בְּהִדָּפָם לָאֳנִיּוֹת

וְתַנִּינִים מְצַפִּים לַסְּעוּדָה

וְעֵת צָרָה כְּמַבְכִּירָה וּבָנִים   15

II Kings 19,3.   Are come to the birth and there is no strength
Isa. 37,3.   to bring forth.
               And though I should lack for food and drink,
               I take the sweetness of Thy name into my
                    mouth for sustenance;
               And I have no care for worldly goods,
               Nor for treasure nor for aught that may
                    perish—
               Even so far that I can forsake her that went
                    forth of my loins,
               Sister of my soul—and she mine only one—
Prov. 7,23.   And I can forget her son, though it pierce my
                    heart,
               And I have nothing left but his memory for a
                    symbol—
               Fruit of my loins, child of my delight—
               Ah! how should Jehudah forget Jehudah?[1]

               But all this is a light thing when set against
                    Thy love,
Ps. 100,4.   Since I may enter Thy gates with thanks-
                    giving,
               And sojourn there, and count my heart
               A burnt offering bound upon Thine altar;
               And may make my grave in Thy land,
Gen. 21,30. So that it be there a witness for me.

---

[1] The poet refers to his only daughter and her **son**
Jehudah, whom he left behind in Spain.

עֲדֵי מַשְׁבֵּר וְאֵין כֹּחַ לְלֵדָה

וְאִלּוּ אֶחֱסַר מַאֲכָל וּמִשְׁתֶּה

נָעִים שִׁמְךָ בְּפִי אָשִׂים לְצֵידָה

וְלֹא אֶדְאַג עֲלֵי קִנְיָן וּבִנְיָן

וְלֹא עַל־הוֹן וְלֹא עַל־כָּל־אֲבֵדָה   20

עֲדֵי כִי אָטְשָׁה יוֹצֵאת חֲלָצַי

אֲחוֹת נַפְשִׁי וְהִיא לִי רַק יְחִידָה

וְאֶשְׁכַּח אֶת־בְּנָהּ פֶּלַח כְּבֵדִי

וְאֵין לִי בִּלְעֲדֵי זִכְרוֹ לְחִידָה

פְּרִי מֵעַי וְיֶלֶד שַׁעֲשׁוּעַי   25

וְאֵיךְ יִשְׁכַּח יְהוּדָה אֶת־יְהוּדָה

וְנָקַל זֹאת לְנֶגֶד אַהֲבָתְךָ

עֲדֵי אָבוֹא שְׁעָרֶיךָ בְּתוֹדָה

וְאָגוּר שָׁם וְאָחֲשֹׁב אֶת־לְבָבִי

עֲלֵי מִזְבַּחֲךָ עוֹלָה עֲקוּדָה   30

וְאֶתֵּן אֶת־קְבוּרָתִי בְּאַרְצֶךָ

לְמַעַן תִּהְיֶה־לִּי שָׁם לְעֵדָה:

12

ON THE SEA

IV

TO THE WEST WIND

This is thy wind, O perfumed west,
With spikenard and apple in his wings!

Thou comest forth of the treasuries of the
    traders in spice—

Ps. 135,7. Thou art not of the treasuries of the wind.
Thou waftest me on swallow's wings, and
    proclaimest liberty for me;

Cant. 1.13. Like pure myrrh from the bundle of spices
    thou art chosen.[1]

How must men long for thee, which for thy sake
Ride over the crest of the sea on the back of a
    plank!

Stay not thine hand from the ship
Either when day abideth or in the cool breath
    of the night;

But beat out the deep, and tear the heart of
    the seas and touch

The holy mountains, and there shalt thou rest.
Rebuke thou the east wind which tosseth the
    sea into tempest

Jer. 1.13. Until he maketh its heart like a seething pot.

     [1] Note the play on the three meanings of the word דרור.

12

משברי ים

IV

לעמת רוח מערבית

‏– – – | – ‎‏‎ ‏– – | – ‎‏‎ – | – ‎‏‎ ‏–‏ ‎‏

זֶה רוּחֲךָ צַד מַעֲרָב רָקוּחַ

הַגֵּרְךָ בִּכְנָפָיו וְהַתַּפּוּחַ

מֵאוֹצְרוֹת הָרְכָלִים מוֹצָאֶךָ

כִּי אֵינְךָ מֵאוֹצְרוֹת הָרוּחַ

כַּנְפֵי דְרוֹר תָּנִיף וְתִקְרָא־לִי דְרוֹר   5

וּכְמָר־דְּרוֹר מִן־הַצְּרוֹר לָקוּחַ

מַה־נִּכְסְפוּ לָךְ עָם אֲשֶׁר בִּגְלָלְךָ

רָכְבוּ בְגַב הַיָּם עֲלֵי נַב־לוּחַ

אַל־נָא תְרַפֶּה יָדְךָ מִן־הָאֳנִי

כִּי יַחֲנֶה הַיּוֹם וְכִי יָפוּחַ   10

וּרְקַע תְּהוֹם וּקְרַע לְבַב יַמִּים וְגַע

אֶל הַרְרֵי־קֹדֶשׁ וְשָׁם תָּנוּחַ

וּגְעַר בְּקָדִים הַמְסָעֵר יָם עֲדֵי

יָשִׂים לְבַב הַיָּם כְּסִיר נָפוּחַ

What shall the captive do, in the hand of God,
One moment held back, and one moment
    sent forth free?

Truly the secret of my quest is in the hand
    of the Highest,
Amos 4.13.   Who formeth the mountain heights and
    createth the wind.

מַה־יַּעֲשֶׂה אָסוּר בְּיַד הַצּוּר אֲשֶׁר
פַּעַם יְהִי עָצוּר וְעֵת שָׁלוּחַ
אַךְ סוֹד שְׁאֵלָתִי בְּיַד מָרוֹם וְהוּא
יוֹצֵר מָרוֹם הָרִים וּבֹרֵא רוּחַ:

13

ON THE SEA

V

My desire for the living God hath constrained
    me
To seek the place of the throne of mine an-
    ointed—

Gen. 31.28. Even so that it hath not suffered me to kiss
The children of my house, my friends, and my
    brethren;
And that I weep not for the orchard which I
    planted
And watered, and my green shoots that
    prospered;
And that I remember not Jehudah and Azariel,
My two beautiful choice flowers;
And Isaac, whom I counted as my child,

Deut. 33.14. Fruit of the sun, best of the growth of my
    moons;
And that I have all but forgotten the house
    of prayer
In whose place of learning was my rest,
And that I forget the delights of my Sabbaths,
The beauty of my Festivals, the glory of my
    Passovers,

Isa. 42.8. And have given my glory unto others,
And forsaken my praise unto graven images.

13

משברי ים

V

‖ ◡ – – ‖ – – ◡ ‖ – – ◡ ‖ – – ◡ ‖

הֲצִיקַתְנִי תְשׁוּקָתִי לְאֵל חָי
לְשַׁחֵר אֶת־מְקוֹם כִּסְאוֹת מְשִׁיחָי
עֲדֵי כִי־לֹא נְטָשַׁתְנִי לְנַשֵּׁק
בְּנֵי בֵיתִי וְאֶת־רֵעַי וְאָחָי
וְלֹא אֶבְכֶּה עֲלֵי פַרְדֵּס נְטַעְתִּיו   5
וְהִשְׁקִיתִיו וְהִצְלִיחוּ צְמָחָי
וְלֹא אֶזְכֹּר יְהוּדָה וַעֲזַרְאֵל
שְׁנֵי פְרָחַי יְקָר מִבְחַר פְּרָחָי
וְאֶת־יִצְחָק אֲשֶׁר כַּבֵּן חֲשַׁבְתִּיו
יְבוּל שִׁמְשִׁי וְטוּב גֶּרֶשׁ יְרָחָי   10
וְכִמְעַט אֶשְׁכְּחָה בֵּית הַתְּפִלָּה
אֲשֶׁר הָיוּ בְמִדְרָשָׁיו מְנוּחָי
וְאֶשְׁכַּח תַּעֲנוּגֵי שַׁבְּתֹתַי
וְהַדְרַת מוֹעֲדַי וּכְבוֹד פְּסָחָי
וְאֶתֵּן אֶת־כְּבוֹדִי לַאֲחֵרִים   15
וְאֶעֱזֹב לַפְּסִילִים אֶת־שְׁבָחָי

I have exchanged mine abode for a shadow of
    shrubs,
And for a hedge in the thicket my strong bars;
And my soul is sated with the chief spices,
And the scent of the thorn-bush is mine now
    for perfume;
And I have ceased to walk with my face
    bending to the ground[1]
But have set my paths in the heart of the
    seas—
To the end that I may find the footstool of
    my God,
And there pour out my soul with my thoughts,
And stand at the threshold of His holy
    mount and set open
Towards the doors of Heaven's gates, my
    doors,
And suffer my spikenard to flower by the
    waters of Jordan,
And put forth my shoots by Siloah.—

The Lord is with me.   How shall I fear or
    dread,
Since the angel of His mercy beareth my
    weapons?
I shall praise His name while yet I live,
And thank Him unto all eternity.

---

[1] In forced servility to man.

הֲמִירוֹתִי בְּצֵל שִׂיחִים חֲדָרַי

וּבְמִשְׂכַּת סְבַךְ חֹסֶן בְּרִיחָי

וְנַפְשִׁי שֶׁבְעָה רָאשֵׁי בְשָׂמִים

וְרֵיחַ נַעֲצוּץ שַׂמְתִּי רְקָחָי   20

וְחָדַלְתִּי הֲלוֹךְ עַל־כַּף וְעַל־אָף

וְנָתַתִּי בְלֵב יַמִּים אֳרָחָי

עֲדֵי אֶמְצָא הֲדֹם רַגְלֵי אֱלֹהַי

וְשָׁמָּה אֶשְׁפְּכָה נַפְשִׁי וְשִׂיחָי

וְאֶסְתּוֹפֵף בְּהַר קָדְשׁוֹ וְאַקְבִּיל   25

לְפִתְחֵי שַׁעֲרֵי־שַׁחַק פְּתָחָי

וְאַפְרִיחַ בְּמֵי יַרְדֵּן נְרָדַי

וְאַשְׁלִיחַ בְּשֻׁלֹּחַ שְׁלָחָי

אֲדֹנִי לִי וְאֵיךְ אִירָא וְאֶפְחַד

וּמַלְאַךְ רַחֲמָיו נֹשֵׂא שְׁלָחָי

אֲהַלֵּל אֶת־שְׁמוֹ מִדֵּי חֲיוֹתִי   30

וְאוֹדֶנּוּ עֲדֵי נֶצַח נְצָחָי׃

14

ON THE SEA

VI

I say in the heart of the seas to the quaking
  heart,

Ps. 93,3. Fearing exceedingly because they lift up their
  waves:

If thou believest in God who made

The sea, and whose Name doth stand unto
  all eternity,

Ps. 89,10. The sea shall not affright thee when the
  waves thereof arise,

Jer. 5,22. For with thee is One who hath set a bound to
  the sea.

14

משברי ים

VI

‏ו – ‎‏ - ‏ | – ‎‏ ‏ - ‏ | – ‏ ‏ ‏ ‏ ‏

אֹמֵר בְּלֵב יַמִּים לְלֵב רַגָּז
חָרֵד מְאֹד כִּי־נָשְׂאוּ דָכְיָם
אִם־תַּאֲמֵן בָּאֵל אֲשֶׁר עָשָׂה
הַיָּם וְעַד־נֶצַח שְׁמוֹ קַיָּם
אַל־יַחֲרִידְךָ יָם בְּשׂוֹא גַלָּיו   5
כִּי־עִמְּךָ הַשֵּׁם נְבוּל לַיָּם:

15

ON THE SEA

VII

Nahum 2,11.   I cry to God with a melting heart and knees
        that smite together,
Is. 21,3.   While anguish is in all loins,
On a day when the oarsmen are astounded at
        the deep,
Ps. 76,6.   When even the pilots find not their hands.
How shall I be otherwise, since I, on a ship's
        deck,
Suspended between waters and heavens,
Ps. 107,27.   Am dancing and tossed about?—But this is
        but a light thing,
Ex. 5,1.   If I may but hold the festal dance in the
Ps. 116,19.   midst of thee, O Jerusalem!

15

משברי ים

VII

‏_ _ | _ ᴗ _ | _ ᴗ _ | _ _ _ ‏

אֶצְעַק בְּלֵב נָמֵס וּפִיק בִּרְכַּיִם
לָאֵל וְחַלְחָלָה בְּכָל־מָתְנַיִם
יוֹם תָּפְשִׂי מָשׁוֹט תְּמַהִים לַתְּהוֹם
גַּם חֹבְלִים לֹא יִמְצְאוּ יָדַיִם
אֵיךְ לֹא־אֶהִי כֵן וַאֲנִי עַל־נֹב אֲנִי
תָּלוּי בְּבֵין מַיִם וּבֵין שָׁמָיִם
אָחוּג וְאָנוּעַ וְנָקֵל זֹאת עֲדֵי
אָחוּג בְּתוֹכֵכִי יְרוּשָׁלָיִם:

16

ON THE SEA

VIII

Call greeting unto daughters and kindred,
Peace to brothers and to sisters,
From the captive of hope who is possessed
By the sea, and hath placed his spirit in the
     hand of the winds,
Thrust by the hand of the west into the hand
     of the east:
This one passeth to lead on, and that one to
     thrust back.

I Sam. 20.3. Between him and death is but a step,
Aye, between them but the thickness of a
     plank;
Buried alive in a coffin of wood,
Upon no floor, with no four cubits of earth,[1]
     nor even with less.

He sitteth—he cannot stand upon his feet,
He lieth down—he cannot stretch them forth;
Sick and afraid because of the heathen
And because of the marauders and the winds.

Job 36,12. The pilot and the mariner, and all their
     rabble—
They are the rulers and captains there.

[1] The minimum amount required for burial.

16

משברי ים

VIII

‖ – ∪ – | – ∪ – | – ∪ – | – –

קָרְאוּ עֲלֵי בָנוֹת וּמִשְׁפָּחוֹת

שָׁלוֹם וְעַל־אַחִים וְעַל־אֲחוֹת

מֵאֵת אֲסִיר תִּקְוָה אֲשֶׁר נִקְנָה

לַיָּם וְשָׂם רוּחוֹ בְּיַד רוּחוֹת

דָּחוּי בְּיַד מַעֲרָב לְיַד מִזְרָח   5

זֶה יַעֲבֹר לַנְחוֹת וְזֶה לִדְחוֹת

בֵּינוֹ וּבֵין מָוֶת כְּפֶשַׂע אַךְ

בֵּינוֹ וּבֵינָיו מַעֲבֵה לוּחוֹת

קָבוּר בְּחַיָּיו בָּאֲרוֹן עֵץ לֹא

קַרְקַע וְלֹא אַרְבַּע וְלֹא פָחוֹת   10

יוֹשֵׁב וְאֵין לַעֲמֹד עֲלֵי רַגְלָיו

שֹׁכֵב וְאֵין רַגְלָיו מְשֻׁלָּחוֹת

חֹלָה וְיָרֵא מִפְּנֵי גוֹיִם

גַּם מִפְּנֵי לִסְטִים וּמֵרוּחוֹת

חֹבֵל וּמַלָּח כָּל־בְּנֵי פִרְחָח   15

הֵם הַסְּגָנִים שָׁם וְהַפַּחוֹת

Eccles. 9,11.

Fame is not to the wise, nor yet favour to
  men of skill,
Save only to them that have skill to swim.
My face is troubled at this for a moment,
(How should the inmost heart exult?)
Until I pour out my soul into the bosom of
  God,
Before the place of the Ark and the altars,
And bestow upon God, who bestoweth good
  things upon the unworthy,
The goodness of songs and praise.

לֹא לַחֲכָמִים שֵׁם וְגַם לֹא חֵן
לַיֹּדְעִים רַק יֹדְעִים לְשֹׁחוֹת
יִתְעַצְּבוּ רָגַע לְזֹאת פָּנַי
אֵיךְ יַעֲלֹז הַלֵּב וְהַטְּחוֹת
עַד אֶשְׁפְּכָה נַפְשִׁי בְּחֵיק הָאֵל
נֹכַח מְקוֹם אָרוֹן וּמִזְבָּחוֹת
אָגְמֹל לְאֵל גְּמֵל לְחַיָּבִים
טוֹבוֹת בְּטוּב שִׁירוֹת וְתִשְׁבָּחוֹת:

17

GLORY UNTO EGYPT

Look on the cities and consider the villages
Which Israel held in possession;
And give glory unto Egypt, and lighten
Thy steps; nay, tread thou not heavily
Ex. 12,12.   Upon the streets where the Divine Presence
         passed through
To seek the blood of the covenant upon the
         doorposts,
Ex. 13,21-22.   And the pillar of fire and the pillars of cloud,
And the eyes of all watching them and be-
         holding!
From thence were hewn the masters of God's
         covenant,
Jud. 20,2.   And thence were carven the corner stones of
         the people of the Lord.

17

כבוד למצרים

‿ – – | ‿ – | ‿ – – | ‿ – |

רְאֵה עָרִים וְהִתְבּוֹנֵן פְּרָזוֹת
אֲשֶׁר הָיוּ לְיִשְׂרָאֵל אֲחֻזּוֹת
וְתֵן כָּבוֹד לְמִצְרַיִם וְהָקֵל
פְּעָמֶיךָ וְאַל־תִּדְרֹךְ עֲזוּזוֹת
בְּחוּצוֹת עָבְרָה בָּם הַשְּׁכִינָה   5
לְבַקֵּשׁ דַּם־בְּרִית עַל־הַמְּזוּזוֹת

וְעַמּוּד אֵשׁ וְעַמּוּדֵי עֲנָנִים
וְעֵינֵי כֹל מְצַפּוֹת בָּם וְחֹזוֹת
וּמִשָּׁם חָצְבוּ בַּעֲלֵי בְרִית־אֵל
וּפְנוֹת עַם־אֲדֹנָי שָׁם גְּרוּזוֹת: 10

18

REFUSAL TO TARRY IN EGYPT

Praise, above all cities, be unto Egypt
Whither came first the word of God.

Ps. 80,9. There a chosen vine was planted,

Whose clusters became a peculiar treasure;

There the envoys of God were born,

Envoys of God, as from bridegroom to bride;

And there God's glory came down and walked

Job 38,9. In a pillar of fire and cloud, swathed in thick
    darkness;

And there the offering of the Lord was made,

And the blood of the covenant given, and
    redemption found.

There stood Moses to supplicate—

And verily no assembly is like unto this for
    prayer.—

And Israel is to be, unto Egypt and Assyria,

Isa. 19,23-24. A third, and a highway between them.

Isa. 19,19. Yea, an altar of the Lord hath been in the
    midst of Egypt,

Neh. 9,5. To exalt His name above all praise,

18

אך לבבי ימאן

‖ – ‿ – | – ‿ – | – ‿ – | – ‿ ‿

לְמִצְרַיִם עֲלֵי כָל-עִיר תְּהִלָּה

אֲשֶׁר הָיָה דְבַר-אֵל שָׁם תְּחִלָּה

וְשָׁמָּה נִטְעָה גֶּפֶן בְּחוּרָה

וְהָיוּ אַשְׁכְּלֹתֶיהָ סְגֻלָּה

וְשָׁם נוֹלְדוּ שְׁלוּחַי אֵל וְהָיוּ   5

שְׁלוּחֵי אֵל כְּבֵין חָתָן וְכַלָּה

וְשָׁם יָרַד כְּבוֹד הָאֵל וְהָלַךְ

בְּעַמּוּד אֵשׁ וְעָנָן וַחֲתֻלָּה

וְשָׁמָּה נַעֲשָׂה קָרְבַּן אֲדֹנָי

וְנִתַּן דַּם-בְּרִית וַיְהִי גְּאֻלָּה   10

וְשָׁמָּה מַעֲמַד מֹשֶׁה לְהַעְתִּיר

וְאֵין מַעֲמָד כְּמוֹ-זֶה לַתְּפִלָּה

וְיִשְׂרָאֵל לְמִצְרַיִם וְאַשּׁוּר

שְׁלִישִׁיָּה וּבֵינוֹתָם מְסִלָּה

וּמִזְבֵּחַ לְאֵל הָיָה בְתוֹכָהּ   15

לְרוֹמֵם אֶת-שְׁמוֹ עַל-כָּל-תְּהִלָּה

And such signs and wonders and fame,
That the world is filled with the glory of His
      memory.
Even her river is of the rivers of Eden,

Lam. 4,2. And the goodness of her soil may be weighed
Gen. 13,10.   against the garden of Eden.

We have tested her, and thus she is—yet my
      heart
Jer. 6,14; 8,11. Refuseth those that give healing so lightly:
For I know that here the Divine Presence
      turned aside,
Jer. 14,8. Like a wayfarer, to the shade of the oak and
      the terebinth,
But in Salem and Zion it is like one home-
      born,
For there is the Torah, there the greatness,
The abode of judgment, the abode of mercy,
And there may a man hope for reward of
      his toil.
Yea, that mountain was called of God the
      Mount of His heritage:
He set it aside for sanctification like the
      hallah.[1]
He came down from the holiness of her unto
      Babylon,
While Egypt was — — — — — — — — —[2]
But when, from any of the lands, a man goeth up
Unto these, highest above the high is she to
      him.

[1] The bread prepared for the sanctuary. See Levit.
24,5, and Num.15,20.
[2] The remainder of the text of this line is missing.

וְהָאֹתֹת וְהַמֹּפְתִים וְהַשֵּׁם

אֲשֶׁר עוֹלָם בְּהוֹד זִכְרוֹ מְמַלֵּא

וְגַם מִנַּהֲרֵי־עֵדֶן נְהָרָה

וְטוּב אַרְצָהּ בְּגַן־עֵדֶן מְסֻלָּא   20

חֲקַרְנוּהָ וְכָהּ־הִיא אַךְ לְבָבִי

יְמָאֵן לַמְרַפְּאִים עַל־נִקְלָה

וְאֵדַע כִּי שְׁכִינָה נֶטְתָה־שָּׁם

כְּאֹרֵחַ לְצֵל אֵלוֹן וְאֵלָה

וְעִם שָׁלֵם וְצִיּוֹן הִיא כְּאֶזְרָח   25

וְשָׁם תּוֹרָה וְשָׁמָּה הַגְּדֻלָּה

מְקוֹם הַדִּין מְקוֹם הָרַחֲמִים שָׁם

וְשָׁם יִחַל אֱנוֹשׁ לִשְׂכַר פְּעֻלָּה

וְהַר נִקְרָא לְאֵל הַר נַחֲלָתוֹ

וְהִפְרִישׁוֹ לְהַקְדִּישׁוֹ כְּחַלָּה   30

וַיֵּרֶד מִקְּדָשָׁתָהּ לְבָבֶל

וּמִצְרָיִם . . . .

אֲבָל אִישׁ יַעֲלֶה מִכֹּל אֲרָצוֹת

אֲלֵיהֶן מַעֲלָה הִיא לוֹ מְעֻלָּה

Then why do the satirists mock at me
And make me a word of reviling?
Since if they believe in God's law
The teaching of Israel refutes them, [1]
And if they lack faith—lo! we part
With no portion in common between us.

Possibly it referred to the conception of the Divine Presence
never returning to Egypt. It has been suggested that
the Egyptian Jews of that time removed the line from the
poem. [Ehrlich reads וְיָרַד in line 31, and supplies in
line 32 the words: כְּמוֹעֵל בָּהּ מְעִילָה. The meaning of
the two lines would then be: He who goes down from
her holiness to Babylon or Egypt is as one committing
against her a trespass. Ed.].

[1] The law against dwelling in Egypt is to be found in
Deut.17,16. This text often caused qualms to the Jewish
communities which settled in Egypt in the Middle Ages.

וְלָמָה יִלְעֲגוּ עָלַי מְלִיצִים

וְלָמָה אֶהְיֶה לָהֶם לְמִלָּה

אֲשֶׁר אִם הֵם בְּדָת־אֵל מַאֲמִינִים

אֲדִינֵמוֹ בְתוֹרַת הַקְּהִלָּה

וְאִם־לֹא יַאֲמִינוּ הֵן מְחִיצָה

וְאֵין בֵּינִי וּבֵינֵיהֶם נָחָלָה:

IN THE WILDERNESS OF EGYPT

19

Fate hath tossed me into the wilderness of
    Memphis:

Isa. 22,17–18. Bid it carry me away and toss me yet again
Until I behold the wilderness of Judah,

Ps. 48,3. And come to the sides of the north, the
    beautiful height,
And I gird me there with glory of the name of
    my God,
And clothe me and veil me with the beauty
    of His holiness.

19

מדברי נף

‎‒‒‒ | ‒ ‒ ‒ | ‒ ‒ ‒ | ‒

צְנָפַנִי זְמָן אֶל מְדַבְּרֵי־נֹף

אֱמֹר לַזְמָן יְטַלְטֵל עוֹד וְיִצְנֹף

עֲדֵי כִי־אֶחֱזֶה מִדַבֵּר יְהוּדָה

וְאָבֹא יַרְכְּתֵי צָפוֹן יְפֵה נֹף

וְאֶעְטָה שָׁם יְקָר מֵשֵּׁם אֱלֹהָי   5

וְאֶלְבַּשׁ אֶת־פְּאַר קָדְשׁוֹ וְאָצְנֹף:

IN THE PATHS OF THE ARK

20

Turn aside with me to Zoan, to the Red Sea,
    to Mount Horeb.
I will go round unto Shiloh to the heap of
    the ruined shrine,
And will get me along in the paths of
    the Ark of the Covenant,
Until I taste the dust of its hiding place
    that is more sweet than honey,
And I see the habitation of that beauteous
    one who hath forgotten her nest,
Since the doves be driven away, and ravens[1]
    abide there.

Because of this my soul is sorely sick and
    grieved,
For through my sin the morn is turned to
    evening time.
Verily, my heart fainteth and longeth for
    the mount of myrrh,
Even as the soul desireth to find its inmost
    home.

[1] עָרָב—Raven or Arab.

20

מסעי ארון הברית

‖ — ⏑ — | — ⏑ — | ⏑ — — | ⏑ — ⏑ —

וְיַם־סוּף וְהַר חֹרֵב	נְטֵה בִי אֱלַי־צַעַן
וְאֶל־תֵּל דְּבִיר חָרֵב	וְאָסֹב אֱלַי שִׁילֹה
אֲרוֹן הַבְּרִית עַד־כִּי	וְאֵלֵךְ אֱלֵי מַסְעַי
אֲשֶׁר מִדְּבַשׁ עָרֵב	אֲלַחֵךְ עֲפַר קִבְרוֹ
אֲשֶׁר שֶׁכְחָה קָנָה	וְאֶרְאֶה נְוֵה נָאוָה 5
וְשָׁכְנוּ בְּנֵי עֶרֶב	וְגֹרְשׁוּ בְּנֵי יוֹנָה
דָּוֶה וְנִכְאָבָה	עֲלֵי־זֹאת מְאֹד נַפְשִׁי
בֹּקֶר לְעֵת עָרֵב	כִּי שָׁב בְּחַטָּאתִי
וְיִכְסוֹף לְהַר הַמּוֹר	לְבָבִי מְאֹד יִכְלֶה
נֶפֶשׁ בְּתוֹךְ קָרֵב:	כַּאֲשֶׁר תְּאַו לִשְׁכֹּן 10

21

ON THE NILE

My God, the wonder of Thee is astir from
    age to age:

Isa. 38,19 From the mouth of father to children no false-
    hood could be told.
And here is the Nile for witness, that Thou
    hast turned it into blood,
Not by magic nor by divination nor by en-
    chantment,
But by Thy name, by the hand of Moses
    and Aaron,
And the staff which was turned into a serpent.

O be a help unto the servant who hath faith
    in Thee,
And who hasteth to behold the places of Thy
    wonder.

21

וזה היאור לעד

‖ – ‿ – | – ‿ – | – ‿ – | – ‿ –

אֱלֹהֵי פְלָאֶךָ דּוֹר דּוֹר יְרָחָשׁ
וּמִפִּי אָב לְבָנִים לֹא־יְכָחָשׁ
וְזֶה הַיְאוֹר לְעַד כִּי־דָם הֲפַכְתּוֹ
בְּלֹא לַהַט וְלֹא קָסָם וְנָחָשׁ
אֲבָל שִׁמְךָ בְּיַד־מֹשֶׁה וְאַהֲרֹן   5
וְהַמַּטֶּה אֲשֶׁר־נֶהְפַּךְ לְנָחָשׁ
הָיָה עֵזֶר לְעָבָד הָאֱמִין בָּךְ
וְלִרְאוֹת אֶת־מְקוֹמוֹת פִּלְאֲךָ חָשׁ:

22

ON EAGLES' WINGS

On the way from Egypt to Zion

Can bodies of clay
  Be prison-houses
For hearts bound fast
  To eagles' wings—
For a man life-weary
  Whose whole desire
Is to lay his face
  In the chosen dust?

Isa. 19,16.   Yet he feared and trembled
  With falling tears,
To cast Spain from him
  And seek shores beyond;
To ride upon ships,
  To tread through wastes,
Dens of lions,

Cant. 4,8.   Mountains of leopards—
But he rebuketh his dear ones
  And chooseth exile,
Forsaketh shelter

Jer. 17,6.   And inhabiteth deserts,
While wolves of the forests
  Find in his sight
The favour of maidens
  In the sight of youths;
And ostriches please him

Ps. 68,26.   Like singers and players,
Zech.11,3. And the roaring of lions
Jud. 5,16.   Like the bleating of flocks;

22

בכנפי נשרים

על דרכו ממצרים ארצה ישראל

‒ ‿ | ‒ ‒ | ‒ ‒ ‖ ‒ ‒ | ‒ ‿ | ‒ ‒ |

הֱיוֹתָם חֲגֵרִים	הֲיוּכְלוּ פְגָרִים
בְּכַנְפֵי נְשָׁרִים	לְלִבּוֹת קְשׁוּרִים
וְכָל־מַאֲוַיָּיו	לְאִישׁ קֵץ בְּחַיָּיו
בְּמִבְחַר עֲפָרִים	לְגַלֵּל לְחָיָיו
וְדָמְעוּ בְמוֹרָד	וּפָחַד וְחָרַד
וְלָתוּר עֲבָרִים	לְהַשְׁלִיךְ סְפָרַד
וְלִדְרֹךְ בְּצִיּוֹת	וְלִרְכֹּב אֳנִיּוֹת
וְהַרְרֵי נְמֵרִים	מְעוֹנוֹת אֲרָיוֹת
וּבָחַר נְדֹדִים	וְנֵעַר בְּדֹדִים
וְשָׁכֵן חֲרָרִים	וְנָטַשׁ חֲדָרִים
זְאֵבֵי יְעָרִים	וּמָצְאוּ בְעֵינָיו
בְּעֵינֵי נְעָרִים	כְּחֵן הַבְּתוּלוֹת
לְשָׁרִים וְנֹגְנִים	וְחָשַׁב יְעֵנִים
שְׁרִקוֹת עֲדָרִים	וְשַׁאֲגַת כְּפִירִים

And he setteth his delight
   In the burnings of his bosom,
And the floods of his tears
   Are like streams of the rivers.
He goeth up by the hills,

Ps. 104,8.

   He goeth down by the valleys,
To perform oaths,
   To fulfil vows;
He journeyeth, he wandereth,
   He passeth by Egypt,
Toward the land of Canaan,
   Toward the chosen of mountains.
The reproofs of his adversaries
   Are renewed round about him,
But he heareth and is silent,

Exod. 4,10.

   Like a man without words;
For how long should he strive with them
   And how long refute them,
And why should he harass them,
   Seeing they are drunken?
But how call him happy
   In the bondage of kings,
Which is in his eyes
   But a service of idols?
Were it well to be happy

Job.1,1; 2,3.

   For a man simple and upright,
Like a bird that is bound
   In the hand of little boys—
In slavery to Philistines,
   And Hagrites and Hittites,[1]
Alluring his heart
   With other gods

[1] Probably indicating Berbers, Mohammedans and Christians.

וְשָׁם שַׁעֲשׁוּעָיו   בְּמוֹקְדֵי צְלָעָיו   15

וּפַלְגֵי דְמָעָיו   כְּפַלְגֵי יְאֹרִים

וַיַּעַל גְּבָעוֹת   וַיֵּרַד בְּקָעוֹת

לְהָקִים שְׁבָעוֹת   וְשַׁלֵּם נְדָרִים

וַיִּסַּע וַיִּצְעַן   וַיַּעֲבֹר בְּצֹעַן

לְאֶרֶץ כְּנַעַן   לְמִבְחַר הֶהָרִים   20

וְתוֹכְחוֹת מְרִיבָיו   חֲלִיפוֹת סְבִיבָיו

וַיִּשְׁמַע וַיַּחֲרִישׁ   כְּלֹא אִישׁ דְּבָרִים

וְכַמָּה יְרִיבֵם   וְכַמָּה יְשִׁיבֵם

וּמַה־יַּעֲצִיבֵם   וְהֵמָּה שְׂכָרִים

וְאֵיךְ אִשְּׁרוּהוּ   בַּעֲבֹדַת מְלָכִים   25

אֲשֶׁר הִיא בְעֵינָיו   עֲבֹדַת אֲשֵׁרִים

הֲטוֹב כִּי־יֵאָשֵׁר   אֱנוֹשׁ תָּם וְיָשָׁר

כְּצִפּוֹר מְקֻשָּׁר   בְּיַד הַצְּעִירִים

בַּעֲבֹדַת פְּלִשְׁתִּים   וְהַגֵּרִים וְחִתִּים

וְלִבּוֹ מְפֻתִּים   אֱלֹהִים אֲחֵרִים   30

To seek their favour
  And forsake God's will,
To betray the Creator
  And serve His creatures?—
The face of the morning
  Would be black to his eyes,[1]
The cup of sweetness
  Bitter to his mouth
Wearied and toiling,
  Oppressed and weak,
And longing for Carmel
  And the City of the Forests,[2]
To seek forgiveness
  At the peaceful graves
Of the ark and the tablets
  That are buried there.—[3]
I shall hope to pass thither,
  I shall fall on their grave,
And mine eyes, at their ruin,
  Shall break forth into torrents,
And all my thoughts
  Trembling unto Sinai,
Mine heart and mine eyes
  Unto Mount Abarim!
And how should I not weep
  And pour forth tears,
And hope therefrom
  The quickening of the dead?
Since there are the Cherubim
  With the written tablets—

Ezek. 47,2.

[1] See the play on words in the Hebrew text.
[2] Kirjath Ye'arim.
[3] Referring to the tradition that the Ark of the Covenant

וְלַעְזֹב רְצוֹן אֵל	לְבַקֵּשׁ רְצוֹנָם
וְלַעֲבֹד יְצוּרִים	וְלִבְגֹּד בְּיֹצֵר
בְּעֵינָיו שְׁחוֹרִים	פְּנֵי הַשְּׁחָרִים
בְּפִיו מַמְרוֹרִים	וְכוֹס מַמְתַּקִים
וְלָחוּץ וְאָמֵל	מִיְגָע וְעָמֵל 35
וְקִרְיַת יְעָרִים	וְנִכְסֹף לְכַרְמֶל
בְּקִבְרֵי מְנוּחוֹת	לְבַקֵּשׁ סְלִיחוֹת
אֲשֶׁר שָׁם קְבָרִים	לְאָרוֹן וְלֻחוֹת
וְאֶעְטֹף בְּקִבְרָם	אֲצַפֶּה לְעָבְרָם
יְפִיצוּן נְהָרִים	וְעֵינַי לְשִׁבְרָם 40
חֲרֵדִים לְסִינַי	וְכָל־רַעְיוֹנַי
לְהַר הָעֲבָרִים	וְלִבִּי וְעֵינַי
וְדֶמַע אַפַּכָּה	וְאֵיךְ לֹא אֲבַכֶּה
תְּחִיַּת פְּגָרִים	וּמִשָּׁם אֲחַכֶּה
וְלֻחוֹת כְּתָבִים	וְשָׁם הַכְּרֻבִים 45

Among the earth clods,
  In a place of secrets,
A place of wonders,
  The fountain of prophecies—
Their faces glowing
  With the glory of God!
I shall fondle its dust
  I shall nestle beside it
And lament upon it
  As over a grave—
And the goal of my thoughts
  To make my couch
'Mid my fathers' graves
  In the demesne of the pure.

Go up, O ship!
  And seek the region
Which hath for the Shekhinah
  Abodes within.
O hasten thy flight
  And God's hand waft thee,
And bind thou thy wings
  To the wings of the dawn—
For them that flee and wander
  With the wind of the sails,
For the hearts that are torn
  To a thousand shreds.
But I am in fear of
  The iniquities of youth,
Those which are counted
  In the scrolls of my God;

was buried before the destruction of the first Temple to save it from exile or desecration.

בְּעַד הֲרַנְבִּים	וּבִמְקוֹם סְתָרִים
מְקוֹם הַפְּלָאוֹת	וְעֵין הַנְּבוּאוֹת
וּבִכְבוֹד צְבָאוֹת	פְּנֵיהֶם מְאִירִים
עָפְרוּ אֶחֱנָן	וְאָצְלוֹ אֶקְנָן
וְעָלָיו אֶקֹנֵן	כְּעַל־הַקְּבָרִים
וְסוֹף מַחְשְׁבוֹתַי	הֱיוֹת מִשְׁכָּבוֹתַי
בְּקִבְרוֹת אֲבוֹתַי	וּבְרָשׁוּת טְהוֹרִים
עֲלֵי הַסְּפִינָה	וְדִרְשֵׁי מְדִינָה
אֲשֶׁר לַשְּׁכִינָה	בְּתוֹכָהּ חֲדָרִים
וְחוּשִׁי בְעוּפָךְ	וְיַד־אֵל תְּנִיפָךְ
וְקִשְׁרִי כְנָפָךְ	בְּכַנְפֵי שְׁחָרִים
לְנָדִים וְנָעִים	בְּרוּחַ קְלָעִים
וְלִבּוֹת קְרָעִים	לְאָלֶף גְּזָרִים
וְיָרֵא אֲנִי מַ־	עֲוֹנוֹת נְעוּרִים
אֲשֶׁר הֵם בְּסִפְרִי	אֱלֹהֵי סְפוּרִים

50

55

60

Yea, more, the iniquities
  Of the days of age,
Changing ever,
Lam. 3,23.   Renewed every morning.
For there is no penitence
  For wantonness—
Gen. 37,30. And whither shall I go
Lam. 1,3.   Between the straits?
I imperil myself,
  By forgetting my trespass,
Whilst my soul and my blood
  Are delivered over to sin.
Yet trust may be drawn
Isa. 55,7.   From Him who is lavish of forgiveness,
And courage and strength
Ps. 68,7.   From the loosener of captives:
And should He judge and punish,
Deut. 4,2.   Award or deprive—
For good or for evil
Berakhoth 54a.   His judgments are right.

וְאַף כִּי־עֲוֹנוֹת   יְמֵי הַזִּקְנוֹת

חֲלִיפוֹת וּמִתְחַד־   דְּשׁוֹת לַבְּקָרִים

וְאֵין־לִי תְשׁוּבָה   בְּעַד הַמְּשׁוּבָה

וְאָנָה אֲנִי־בָא   בְּבֵין הַמְּצָרִים

אֶסָּכֵן בְּעַצְמִי   וְאֶשְׁכַּח אֲשָׁמִי   65

וְנַפְשִׁי וְדָמִי   בְּיַד־חַטָּא מְסוּרִים

אֲבָל יֵשׁ בְּטֹחַ   בְּמַרְבָּה סָלֹחַ

וְחַיִל וְכֹחַ   לְמוֹצִיא אֲסִירִים

וְאִם דָּן וְנִפְרָע   וְיוֹסִיף וְיִגְרַע

עֲלֵי־טוֹב וְעַל־רָע   שְׁפָטָיו יְשָׁרִים: 70

II. LOVE AND BRIDAL SONGS

23

A SLAVE TO LOVE

By the life of our troth, my love, by thy life
    and the life
Of love which hath shot an arrow at me,
Ex. 21.6.   Verily have I become a slave to Love, that
    hath pierced
Mine ear, that hath cloven my heart in twain.

23

עבד לאהבה

‎– ‎∪ – ‎| – ‎∪ – ‎| – ‎∪ – ‎| – ‎∪ –

חֵי הַבְּרִית דּוֹדִי וְחַיָּיךְ וְחֵי
הָאַהֲבָה שֶׁיָּרְתָה בִּי חֵצִי
אִם־לֹא אֱהִי עֶבֶד לְאַהֲבָה רֶצְעָה
אָזְנִי וְלִבִּי בְּתֶרָה בַּחֲצִי:

24

PARTED LOVERS

Isa. 57.9.   Wherefore, O fair one, dost withhold thy
          messengers
Isa. 13.8.   From the lover whose frame is filled with the
          pains of thee?

Knowest thou not that thy lover awaiteth
      nothing from fate
But to hear the voice of thy greeting?

If parting be decreed for the two of us,
Ps. 17.15.   Stand yet a little, while I gaze upon thy face.

I know not if my heart be held back within
      my frame
Gen. 13.3.   Or if it goeth forth upon thy wanderings.

By the life of love, remember the days of
      thy longing, as I—
I remember the nights of thy delight.

As thine image passeth into my dream,
So let me pass, I entreat thee, into thy dreams.

Isa. 51.15. Jer.   Between me and thee roar the waves of a sea
31.34.   of tears
And I cannot pass over unto thee.

But O if thy steps should draw nigh to cross—

24

הפרידה

‏– – | – ‑ – | – – | – ‑ – |

מַה־לָּךְ צְבִיָּה תִּמְנְעִי צִירַיִךְ
מִדּוֹד צְלָעָיו מָלְאוּ צִירַיִךְ
לֹא תֵדְעִי כִּי־אֵין לְדוֹדֵךְ מִזְמָן
בִּלְתִּי שְׁמֹעַ קוֹל שְׁלֹמוֹתָיִךְ
אִם הַפְּרִידָה עַל־שְׁנֵינוּ נִגְזְרָה   5
עָמְדִי מְעַט עַד־אֶחֱזֶה פָּנָיִךְ
לֹא אֵדְעָה אִם בֵּין צְלָעַי נֶעֱצַר
לִבִּי וְאִם יֵלֵךְ לְמַסָּעָיִךְ
חַי אַהֲבָה זִכְרִי יְמֵי חִשְׁקֵךְ כְּמוֹ
אֶזְכֹּר אֲנִי לֵילוֹת תְּשׁוּקוֹתָיִךְ   10
כַּאֲשֶׁר דְּמוּתֵךְ בַּחֲלוֹמִי יַעֲבֹר
כֵּן אֶעְבְּרָה־נָּא בַּחֲלֹמוֹתָיִךְ
בֵּינִי וּבֵינֵךְ יָם דְּמָעוֹת יָהֱמוּ
גַּלָּיו וְלֹא־אוּכַל עֲבֹר אֵלָיִךְ
אַךְ לוּ פְעָמַיִךְ לְעָבְרוֹ קֵרְבוּ   15

Then would its waters be divided at the touch
    of thy foot.

Would that after my death, unto mine ears
    should come

Ex. 28.33–34. The sound of the golden bells upon thy skirts![1]
Ex.39,25–26

Or shouldst thou be asking how fareth thy
    belovèd, I from the depths of the tomb
Would ask of thy love and thy welfare.

Deut. 21,7. Verily, to thy shedding of mine heart's blood
Deut. 17,6. There be two witnesses—thy cheeks and
    thy lips.

How sayest thou it is not true, since these be
    my witnesses
For my blood, and that thine hands have
    shed it?

Why desirest thou my death, whilst I but
    desire
To add years unto the years of thy life?

Prov. 4,16. Though thou dost rob my slumber in the night
Isa. 21,4.   of my longing,
Would I not give the sleep of mine eyes unto
    thine eyelids?

I Kings 18,38. The fire of thee licketh up the waters of tears,
Job 14,19. Yea, and the waters of thy tears wear the
Ezek. 11,19   hearts of stone.

    [1] The poet refers to the bells on the skirts which are
still worn in old-fashioned countries of the Orient, and
also in Spain.

אָז נִבְקְעוּ מֵימָיו לְכַף רַגְלָיִךְ

לוּ אַחֲרֵי מוֹתִי בְּאָזְנַי יַעֲלֶה

קוֹל פַּעֲמֹן זָהָב עֲלֵי שׁוּלָיִךְ

אוֹ תִשְׁאֲלִי לִשְׁלוֹם יְדִידַךְ מִשְׁאוֹל

אֶשְׁאַל בְּדוֹדַיִךְ וּבִשְׁלָמָיִךְ   20

אָכֵן עֲלֵי שָׁפְכֵךְ דְּמֵי לִבִּי שְׁנֵי

עֵדִים לְחָיַיִךְ וְשִׂפְתוֹתָיִךְ

אֵיךְ תֹּאמְרִי לֹא־כֵן וְהֵם עֵדַי עֲלֵי

דָמִי וְעַל־כִּי שֻׁפְּכוּ יָדָיִךְ

מַה־תֶּחְפְּצִי מוֹתִי וְהֵן אֶחְפֹּץ אֲנִי   25

שָׁנִים לְהוֹסִיף עֲלֵי־שְׁנֵי חַיָּיִךְ

אִם־תִּגְזְלִי נוּמִי בְּלֵיל חִשְׁקִי הֲלֹא

אֶתֵּן שְׁנָת עֵינַי לְעַפְעַפָּיִךְ

מֵימֵי דְמָעוֹת לַחֲכָה אֶשָּׁךְ וְנָם

אַבְנֵי לְבָבוֹת שָׁחֲקוּ מֵימָיִךְ   30

Ps. 66,12.   But now I come into the fire of longing for
          thee and the torrents of my weeping!
      Alas, my heart! between my tears and thy
          glowing coals!

      Yea, between the bitter and the sweet standeth
          my heart—
      The gall of parting, and the honey of thy
          kisses.

Ex. 39,3.   After thy words have beaten out my heart into
          thin plates,
      Thine hands have cut it into shreds.

Ezek.1,26,28.   It is the likeness of rubies over pearls
      What time I behold thy lips over thy teeth.

      The sun is on thy face and thou spreadest
          out the night
      Over his radiance with the clouds of thy locks.

Ezek. 16,13.   Fine silk and broidered work are the covering
Gen. 20,16.   of thy body,
      But grace and beauty are the covering of
          thine eyes.

      The adornment of maidens is the work of
          human hands,
Isa. 2,16.   But thou—majesty with sweetness are thine
          adornment.

Job 9,9.   Sun and moon, the Plough and the Pleiads
          are zealous
      To be brothers and sisters of thine;

בָּאתִי בְּאֵשׁ חֶשְׁקֵךְ וּמֵי בִכְיִי אָהָה

לִבִּי בְדִמְעוֹתִי וְנֶחֱלָיִךְ

בֵּין מַר וּמָתוֹק יַעֲמֹד לִבִּי וְהֵם

רֹאשׁ הַנֶּדֶד וּדְבַשׁ נְשִׁיקוֹתָיִךְ

אַחֲרֵי דְבָרַיִךְ כְּפַחִים רֻקְּעוּ   35

אֹתוֹ פְּתִילִם קִצְּצוּ יָדָיִךְ

מַרְאֵה דְמוּת אֹדֶם עֲלֵי סַפִּיר בְּעֵת

אֶרְאֶה שְׂפָתַיִךְ עֲלֵי שִׁנָּיִךְ

שֶׁמֶשׁ בְּפָנַיִךְ וְלַיְל תִּפְרְשִׂי

עַל־זָהֳרוֹ עָבֵי קְוֻצּוֹתָיִךְ   40

מֶשִׁי וְרִקְמָה הֵם כְּסוּת גּוּפֵךְ אֲבָל

הַחֵן וְהַיֹּפִי כְּסוּת עֵינָיִךְ

מַשְׂכִּית עֲלָמוֹת מַעֲשֵׂה יַד־אִישׁ וְאַתְּ

הַהוֹד וְהַחֶמְדָּה שְׂכִיּוֹתָיִךְ

חֶרֶס וְסַהַר עָשׂ וְכִימָה קִנְּאוּ   45

לִהְיוֹת כְּאַחַיִךְ וַאֲחִיּוֹתָיִךְ

Men and maidens think, ah! would they were
    but free
To be thy slaves and thine handmaidens!

As for my share of worldly wealth, I ask for
    nought
Gen. 14,23.   But a thread of scarlet from thy lips, a girdle
    from thy waist.

Cant.5,1.   My sweet wild honey is between thy lips,
Cant. 4.14.   My spikenard and my myrrh between thy
    breasts.

Jer. 22,24.   I have placed thee as a seal upon my right
    hand; O would that I too
Cant. 8.6.   Might be as a seal upon thine arms.

Ps. 137,5.   May I forget to discern my right hand from
Jonah 4,11.   my left, O my doe,
Jer. 2,2.   If I ever forget the love of thine espousals.

Separation maketh my heart bitter, when I
    remember
Upon my lips the sweet honey of thy kisses.

Ex. 22,15.   With the fragrance of thy pure myrrh will I
Ex. 30,23.   endow me with fragrance:
Then perchance, through my fragrance, I
    may kiss thy lips.

Lo, the glory of women is the praise of them—
    but thou—
Thy praises draw glory from thee.

בָּנִים וּבָנוֹת חָשְׁבוּ אִם חָפֵשׁוּ

לִהְיוֹת עֲבָדֶיךָ וְשִׁפְחוֹתָיִךְ

לֹא־אֶשְׁאֲלָה מֵהוֹן זְמָן חֶלְקִי לְבַד

מָחוּט שְׂפָתַיִךְ חֲגוֹר מָתְנָיִךְ

יַעְרִי וְדִבְשִׁי בֵּין שְׂפָתַיִךְ כְּמוֹ

נִרְדִּי וּמֹרִי בֵּין שְׁנֵי שָׁדָיִךְ

שַׂמְתִּיךְ כְּחוֹתָם עַל־יְמִינִי לוּ אֲנִי

אֶהְיֶה כְחוֹתָם עַל־זְרֹעוֹתָיִךְ

אֶשְׁכַּח יְמִינִי מִשְּׂמֹאלִי יַעֲלָה

אִם־אֶשְׁכָּחָה אַהֲבַת כְּלוּלֹתָיִךְ

הֲמַר נָדֹד לִבִּי בְּזָכְרִי יַעֲרַת

נֹפֶת שְׂפָתַי מִנְּשִׁיקוֹתָיִךְ

רֵיחִי בְּרֵיחַ מָר־דְּרוֹרַךְ אָמְהֲרָה

אוּלַי בְּרֵיחִי אֶשְׁקָה אַפָּיִךְ

הִנֵּה כְבוֹד נָשִׁים תְּהִלָּתָן וְאַתְּ

בָּךְ נִכְבְּדוּ הַיּוֹם תְּהִלּוֹתָיִךְ

In the field of the daughters of delight, the
    sheaves of love

Gen. 37.7. Make obeisance unto thy sheaf.

Cant. 5.1. Would that I might live until I had gathered
Spices and myrrh from amid thy footprints.

II Sam.5.24. I cannot hear thy voice, but I hear
I Chron. 14,15. Upon the secret places of my heart, the sound
    of thy steps.

Ex. 32,34. On the day when thou wilt revive
Isa. 26,19 The victims whom love for thee hath slain—
    on the day when thy dead shall live anew,

Then turn again to my soul to restore it to
    my body; for on the day
Of thy departure, when thou wentest forth, it
    went out after thee.

Ask, O doe of grace, for the peace of thy
    lover,
Should Time ask of thee thy request.

Ps. 107,30. Return, so our God shall restore thee to the
    haven
Ezek. 21,35; Of thy desire, and to the land of thy true
16,3; 29,14.   belonging.

בִּשְׂדָה בְּנוֹת חֶשֶׁק אֱלְמוֹת אַהֲבָה
תִּשְׁתַּחֲוֶיןָ, לְאַלְמוֹתָיִךְ
מִי־יִתְּנֵנִי אֶחֱיֶה עַד־אֶאֱרֶה 65
בְּשָׂם וָמֹר מִבֵּין הֲלִיכוֹתָיִךְ
לֹא־אֶשְׁמְעָה קוֹלֵךְ אֲבָל אֶשְׁמַע עֲלֵי
סִתְרֵי לְבָבִי קוֹל צְעָדוֹתָיִךְ
פִּקְדִי בְּיוֹם פָּקְדֵךְ לְחַיּוֹת חֲלָלַי
חִשְׁקֵךְ וְיוֹם בּוֹ יָחְיוּ מֵתָיִךְ 70
נַפְשִׁי לְהָשִׁיב אֶל־גְּוִיָּתִי בְּיוֹם
נָסְעֵךְ בְּצֵאתֵךְ יֵצְאָה אַחֲרָיִךְ
בִּשְׁלוֹם יְדִידַךְ יַעֲלַת־חֵן שַׁאֲלִי
אִם הַזְּמָן יִשְׁאַל שְׁאֵלוֹתָיִךְ
שׁוּבִי וְצוּרֵנוּ יְשִׁיבֵךְ אֶל־מְחוֹז 75
חֶפְצֵךְ וְאֶל־אֶרֶץ מְכוֹרוֹתָיִךְ:

25

OPHRA

Ophra washeth her garments in the waters
Of my tears, and spreadeth them out in the
    sunshine of her radiance.
She demandeth no water of the fountains,
    having my two eyes;
And no other sunshine than her beauty.

25

עפרה

‒ ‒ | ‒ ‒ | ‒ ‒ | ‒ ‒ |

עָפְרָה תְּכַבֵּס אֶת־בְּגָדֶיהָ בְּמֵי
דִּמְעִי וְתִשְׁטָחֵם לְשֶׁמֶשׁ זָהֳרָה
לֹא שָׁאֲלָה מֵי הָעֲיָנוֹת עִם שְׁתֵּי
עֵינַי וְלֹא שֶׁמֶשׁ לְיֹפִי תָאֲרָהּ:

26

CHOSEN OF BRIDEGROOMS

Carry ye greeting to the chosen of bridegrooms
And his loved ones and faithful friends—
The greeting of a lover who overcometh the
    distance with his eyes,
And seeth with his heart, face to face,
When the two children of princes are joined,
Isa. 17,10; 32,5. Children of nobles, plants of loveliness,
Whose faces give light through the marriage
    bower
Like stars through the thickness of clouds.

26

למבחר החתנים

‖ – – – | – – ‿ | – – – ‿

שְׂאוּ שָׁלוֹם לְמִבְחַר הַחֲתָנִים
וְאֶל־דּוֹדִים וְרֵעִים נֶאֱמָנִים
שְׁלוֹם דּוֹד יָחֱזֶה רָחוֹק בְּעֵינָיו
וְלִבּוֹ יָחֱזֶה פָּנִים בְּפָנִים
בְּהִתְחַבֵּר שְׁנֵי יַלְדֵי נְדִיבִים
בְּנֵי שׁוֹעִים וְנִטְעֵי נַעֲמָנִים
וְיָאִירוּ בְּעַד חֻפָּה פְּנֵיהֶם
כְּכוֹכָבִים בְּעַד עַב הָעֲנָנִים:

5

27

AMID THE MYRTLES

The bridal pair stand amid the myrtles,
Sending forth pure myrrh on every side.
The myrtle desireth the sweetness of their
    fragrance,
And spreadeth his wings like a cherub above
    them.
The myrtle thinketh to cover their fragrance,
But the sweetness of their spices overwhelmeth
    his scent.

27

בין ההדסים

‏ ‏ | ‏ ‏ | ‏ ‏ | ‏ ‏

עֲפָרִים עָמְדוּ בֵּין הַהֲדַסִּים

דְּרוֹר מֹר שֶׁלְחוּ אֶל־הָאֲפָסִים

הֲדַס חָמַד נְעִים רֵיחָם וְנָתַן

כְּנָפָיו כַּכְּרוּב בְּעָדָם פְּרָשִׂים

יְדַמֶּה הַהֲדַס רֵיחָם לְכַסּוֹת

וּבִשְׂמֵיהָם עֲלֵי רֵיחוֹ מְכַסִּים:

5

28

WHY RISEST THOU, O SUN

Why risest thou, O sun, why shinest thou?
The turn of Abihail's daughter[1] hath come.
She shameth the face of the sun with the
    splendour of her form,
She hindereth the host of heaven from their
    work.
She chooseth not to dwell in the heavens above,
But maketh her heaven of the myrtle tree.

Es. 2,15.

---

[1] Esther, the daughter of Abiḥail, whose name was
also Hadassah, *i. e.* Myrtle.

28

מה תעלה שמש

‏– ‿ – | ‿ – | ‿ – | ‿ – ‿ ‿ |

מַה־תַּעֲלֶה שֶׁמֶשׁ וּמַה־תּוֹפִיעַ
תֹּר בַּת־אֲבִיחַיִל כְּבָר הִגִּיעַ
תַּחְפִּיר פְּנֵי־שֶׁמֶשׁ בְּזֹהַר תָּאֳרָהּ
וּצְבָא זְבָל מִמַּעֲשָׂיו תַּפְרִיעַ
לֹא־בָחֲרָה לִשְׁכֹּן רְקִיעֵי מַעֲלָה
וַתַּעֲשֶׂה מִן־הֲדַדס רָקִיעַ:

5

29

THE FAIR MAIDEN

The night when the fair maiden revealed the
    likeness of her form to me,
The warmth of her cheeks, the veil of her hair,
Golden like a topaz, covering
A brow of smoothest crystal—
She was like the sun making red in her rising
The clouds of dawn with the flame of her
    light.

29

צביה

‒ ∪ ‒ | ‒ ∪ ‒ | ∪ ‒ ∪ | ‒ ‒

לֵיל גִּלְּתָה אֵלַי צְבִיָּה נַעֲרָה
חַמַּת לְחָיֶיהָ וְצַמַּת שַׂעֲרָה
צָהֹב כְּעֵין אֹדֶם בְּכַסּוֹתוֹ עֲלַי
רַקַּת בְּדֹלַח לַח תְּמוּנַת תָּאֳרָה
דָּמְתָה כְשֶׁמֶשׁ בַּעֲלֹתָהּ תַּאֲדִים
אֶת־עֲנָנֵי נֶשֶׁף בְּלַהַב זָהֲרָה:

5

30

BY AN APPLE TREE

I lift my greeting on the wings of the wind
Cant. 2,17. To my friend, when the heat of the day be-
    ginneth to cool.
I ask him nought but to remember the day
    of our parting,
When we made a covenant of love by an
    apple tree.

30

עלי תפוח

‏‎‏- – ‏ ‎‎ – ‏ – | ‏ ‎ – ‏ – | ‏ ‎ – ‏ –

אֶשָּׂא שְׁלוֹמִי עַל־כְּנַף הָרוּחַ
אֶל־דּוֹד כְּחֹם הַיּוֹם בְּעֵת יָפוּחַ
לֹא־אֶשְׁאֲלָה בִּלְתִּי זְכֹר יוֹם הַנְּדֹד
בִּכְרֹת בְּרִית אַהַב עֲלֵי תַפּוּחַ:

31

THE MEETING OF THE STARS

The stars of the world have joined to-day.
'Mid the host on high none are found like
    these.
The Pleiads desire such unity,

Job 41,8.   For no breath can come between them.
The star of the east hath come to the west;
He hath found the sun among the daughters
    thereof.
He hath set up a bower of thick branches;

Ps. 19,5.   He hath made of them a tent for the sun.

31

כוכבי תבל

— — — —

כּוֹכְבֵי תֵבֵל כַּיּוֹם חֻבְּרוּ
בִּצְבָא רוֹם לֹא נִמְצָא כָהֶם
חָמְדָה כִימָה חַבְרָתָם כִּי
רוּחַ לֹא־יָבֹא בֵּינֵיהֶם
כּוֹכַב מִזְרָח בָּא לַמַּעְרָב   5
מָצָא שֶׁמֶשׁ בִּגְבוּלֹתֵיהֶם
הֵקִים חֻפַּת עַנְפֵי עָבוֹת
לַשֶּׁמֶשׁ שָׁם אֹהֶל בָּהֶם:

32

THE DAUGHTER OF THE DAWN

Look if the daughter of the dawn hath rent
The blackness of her armour,
At the sound of the maiden's songs,
At the sound of the song of her doves.

Amos 7.16.   What word shall I drop on the house of Isaac—
The branch that is like to the root?[1]
On the brow of the days it is graven
That he inheriteth dominion;
A man seeketh to ascend to the clouds
If he should seek to acquire it.

Whether it please or anger them,
Say unto them who would get it:
Turn—for the heritage of dominion
Ex. 21.4.   Belongeth to her masters.

Perfumes from far off lands
Have ridden on the wings of the wind;
The scent of purest spices
From the graceful doe they have stolen,
Ps. 55.15.   For her sake taking sweet counsel together,
For the times of love draw nigh.

Come down, her belovèd—why tarriest thou
To feed amid her gardens?
Cant. 6.2.   Turn aside to the couch of love,
To gather her lilies.

    [1] The son that is like the sire.

32

בת שחר

‒ ‒ ‒ ‒ ‒ | ‒ ‒ ‒ ‒ ‒ ‒

שַׁחֲרוּת שְׂרִיּוֹנֶיהָ   שׁוּר אִם קָרְעָה בַּת־שַׁחַר
וּלְקוֹל שִׁיר יוֹנֶיהָ:   אַל־קוֹל שִׁירֵי הַנַּעֲרָה

מָה אַטִּיף עַל־בֵּית יִשְׂחָק עָנָף דּוּמָה שֹׁרֶשׁ
עַל־מֵצַח יָמִים הוּחַק   כִּי הוּא מִשְׂרָה יוֹרֵשׁ
יִדְרשׁ לַעֲלוֹת אֶל־שַׁחַק   אִישׁ לִקְנוֹתָהּ דֹּרֵשׁ   5

אָמְרוּ אֶל־קוֹנֶיהָ   יִיטַב לָהֶם אוֹ יֵחַר
תִּהְיָה לַאדוֹנֶיהָ:   שׁוּבוּ כִּי נַחֲלַת מִשְׂרָה

כַּנְפֵי־רוּחַ רָכְבוּ   מָרְקָחִים מִמֶּרְחַקִּים
מִיַּעֲלַת־חֵן גֻּנְּבוּ   רֵיחַ בָּשְׂמֵי תַמְרוּקִים
בַּעֲבוּרָהּ סוֹד מַמְתִּיקִים   עִתּוֹת דּוֹדִים קָרְבוּ   10

לִרְעוֹת תּוֹךְ גַּנֶּיהָ   דּוֹדָהּ רַד מַה־תִּתְאַחַר
לַלְקֹט שׁוֹשַׁנֶּיהָ:   לַעֲרוּגַת אַהֲבָה סוּרָה

Sweet apples of her breasts
Cant. 7,14.   Give forth their fragrance;
For thee she hideth in her necklaces
Precious fruits shining like light:
Wait a little for her precious fruits
Until the moon be full.

For full-moon it will be tomorrow—
Like one of the moons of her adornment,
And to thee she will be a lamp,
Lighting up her bowers.

Beautiful is thy fair gazelle—
Isa. 30,26.   Her light is sevenfold;
She would shame, but for her veil,
All the stars of heaven.
Pomegranates upon a watered branch—
Guard them from other eyes!

Though she bring her serpents forth
From behind her veil,
Thou shalt have no fear of them:
Her adders have no venom.

Cant. 4,6.   The soul of the hill of frankincense
Thirsteth for the mountain of myrrh,
Hos. 2,22.   Until he have betrothed her to himself in
faithfulness,
Ps. 84.4.   And the swallow hath found her a nest.
Cant. 6,10.   Pure and fair as the moon—
All praise faileth to tell of her.

The dawn of her countenance darkeneth
Job 38,32.   The Great Bear and his train;
And a lamp of grace she lighteth
Ex. 25,37.   Before her face.

הַיּוֹם נָתְנוּ רֵיחַ   דּוּדָאִים מְדַדָּיִךְ

מֶנֶּד אוֹר זְרַח   לָךְ תִּצְפּוֹן בְּרָבִידָיִךְ

עַד יִשְׁלַם יָרַח   יַחַל קָט לְמַגְדַּיִךְ   15

חַד מִשַּׁהֲרֹנָיִךְ   כִּי סַהַר יִהְיֶה מָחָר

תָּאִיר מִשְׁכְּנָיִךְ:   וּלָךְ תִּהְיֶה לִמְנוֹרָה

אוֹרָה שִׁבְעָתָיִם   נָאוָה לָךְ עָפְרַת נָוֶה

כָּל־כּוֹכְבֵי שָׁמַיִם   הָחָפִירָה לוּלֵי מַסְוֵה

שָׁמְרָה מֵעֵינָיִם   רָמֵּנִי סָעִיף רָוֶה   20

צָעִיף צִפְעוֹנָיִךְ   כִּי הוֹצִיאָה מֵאַחַר

אֵין רוֹשׁ בְּפִתְנָיִךְ:   אַךְ אַתְּ מֵהֶם אַל תִּירָא

אַל־הֵר הַמּוֹר צְמָאָה   נֶפֶשׁ גִּבְעַת הַלְּבוֹנָה

וּדְרוֹר קֵן לָהּ מָצָאָה   עַד אַרְשָׂה לּוֹ בֶּאֱמוּנָה

כָּל־מַהֲלָל בָּהּ נִלְאָה   בָּרָה יָפָה כַלְּבָנָה   25

עַיִשׁ עַל־בָּנֶיהָ   שַׁחַר פָּנַיִךְ שַׁחַר

אַל עֵבֶר פָּנֶיךָ:   וּמְנוֹרַת חֵן הָאִירָה

33

TO THE BRIDEGROOM

(For rhymed version see page 159)

Eccl. 11,9.   Rejoice, O young man in thy youth,
And gather the fruit of thy joy,
Thou and the wife of thy youth
Ruth 4,11.   Who cometh to thine house.

Precious blessings of the only God
Deut.33,16.   Shall come upon thine head together,
Job 21,9.   And thine house shall be at peace from dread,
And all who rise against thee shall be cut off.
And when thou liest down thou shalt not be
afraid;
Prov. 3,24.   Thou shalt lay thee down and thy sleep
be sweet.

Ps. 45,5.   In thine honour, my bridegroom, ride on and
prosper,
Raise up and put forth thy beauty;
And the heart of thine enemies God shall
pierce,
And the sins of thy youth He will forgive,
And will bless thee in all the doings
Deut. 28,20.   Of thine hand and in all thine increase.
Deut. 16,15.

Eccl. 12,1.   And remember thy Rock and thy Creator
When the good cometh which He shall bring
thee,

33

שמח בחור

— — — — — — | — — — — —

שְׂמַח בָּחוּר בְּיַלְדוּתֶךָ   וָאֱרֶה פְּרִי שִׂמְחָתֶךָ
אַתָּה וְאֵשֶׁת נְעוּרֶיךָ   הַבָּאָה אֶל־בֵּיתֶךָ:

יָקָר בִּרְכַּת אֵל מְיָחָד
תְּבוֹאתָה לְרֹאשְׁךָ יַחַד
וּבֵיתְךָ שָׁלוֹם מִפַּחַד
וְכָל־מִתְקוֹמֵם בְּךָ נִכְחָד

וְאִם־תִּשְׁכַּב לֹא־תִפְחָד   וְשָׁכַבְתָּ וְעָרְבָה שְׁנָתֶךָ:

הֲדָרְךָ חֲתָנִי רֶכֶב וּצְלַח
וְתִפְאַרְתְּךָ הַעֲלֵה וְשֶׁלַח
וְלֵב אֹיְבֶיךָ אַל יִפְלַח
וְחַטֹּאת נְעוּרֶיךָ יִסְלַח

וִיבָרֶכְךָ בְּכֹל מִשְׁלַח   יָדֶךָ וְכָל־תְּבוּאָתֶךָ:

וְזָכַר צוּרְךָ וּבוֹרַאֲךָ
בְּעֵת מְבוֹא הַטּוֹב יְבִיאֲךָ

For children, in course of the days, shall
    come to thee,

Deut. 33,25. And as thy days, so shall thy strength be.
Blessed be thou in thy coming in
Deut. 28,6.   And blessed be thou in thy going out.

Thy word shall be with men of perfection,
So thou be discreet wherever thou turn;
And thine house shall be firmly builded,
Isa. 58,9. And "Peace," thou shalt call and God shall
    reply,
And peace shall be thine habitation, and with
    the stones
Job 5,23.   Of the field thy covenant.

Thine honour shall ascend, and tarry not,
And thee shall He call, yea, shall choose,
And thy light in the night and the gloom
Isa. 58,8. Then shall break through like the dawn;
And for thee, from the womb of the morning,
Ps. 110,3.   The dew of thy youth!

כִּי בְנֵי יָמִים יְבוֹאוּךָ   15
וּכְיָמֶיךָ דָּבְאֶךָ

בָּרוּךְ אַתָּה בְּבֹאֶךָ   וּבָרוּךְ אַתָּה בְּצֵאתָךָ:

דְּבָרְךָ בְּמָתַי תֹם תִּקְנֶה
לְמַעַן תַּשְׂכִּיל בְּכֹל תִּפְנֶה
וּבֵיתְךָ יִכּוֹן וְיִבָּנֶה   20
וְשָׁלוֹם תִּקְרָא וְאַל יַעֲנֶה

וְשָׁלוֹם נְוָתְךָ וְעִם־אַבְנֵי   הַשָּׂדֶה בְרִיתָךָ:

הוֹדְךָ יַעֲלֶה וְלֹא יְאַחַר
וְאוֹתְךָ יִקְרָא גַּם יִבְחַר
וְאוֹרְךָ בְּלֵילוֹת וָשַׁחַר   25
אָז יִבָּקַע כַּשַּׁחַר

וּלְךָ מֵרָחָם מִשְׁחָר   טַל יַלְדֻתָךָ:

34

AMID THE TREES OF EDEN

Thou who, amid the trees of Eden, art a
    flowering myrtle tree,
And amid the stars of heaven, art the bright
    Orion,
God hath sent to thee a cluster of pure myrrh
Of His own work, not the perfumer's skill.

The dove from whom, that day she nested
    in the myrtle tree,
The myrtle stole her fragrance and gave forth
    perfume—
Ask not, while with her, for the sun to rise;
She asketh not, with thee, for the rising of the
    moon.

34

בֵּין עֲצֵי עֵדֶן

‒ ‒ ∪ ‒ | ∪ ‒ | ∪ ∪ ‒ | ∪ ‒ ‒ ‖

אַתְּ בֵּין עֲצֵי־עֵדֶן הֲדַס פֹּרֵחַ
וּבְכוֹכְבֵי שַׁחַק כְּסִיל זֹרֵחַ
שָׁלַח לְךָ הָאֵל צְרוֹר מִמָּר־דְּרוֹר
מִמַּעֲשָׂיו לֹא מַעֲשֵׂה רֹקֵחַ
יוֹנָה אֲשֶׁר יוֹם קִנְּנָה בֵּין הַהֲדַס
גָּנַב הֲדַס רֵיחָהּ וְנָתַן רֵיחַ

5

אַל־תִּשְׁאֲלָה עִמָּהּ עֲלוֹת שֶׁמֶשׁ כְּמוֹ
לֹא־שָׁאֲלָה עִמָּךְ עֲלוֹת יָרֵחַ:

35

UNTO THE STARS TO REACH THEE

Would that morning might pursue me with
    the wind
That kisseth her mouth and swayeth her body;
And would the clouds might bear to her my
    greeting—
Then, like her frame, so would the hardness
    of her heart be moved.
Thou gazelle, that choosest to rest upon the
    stars[1],
Have pity upon him who must fly unto the
    stars to reach thee.

[1] The Bear.

35

עֲדִי עָשׁ יְעוֹפֵף

‒ ᵕ ‒ ‒ | ‒ ᵕ ‒ | ‒ ᵕ ‒ |

לוּ שְׁחָרִים יִרְדְּפוּנִי בְרוּחַ
הַמְנַשֵּׁק פִּיהָ וְגוּפָהּ יְנוֹפֵף
וַעֲנָנִים לוּ נָשְׂאוּ לָהּ שְׁלוֹמִי
אָז כְּמָתְנָהּ קְשִׁי לְבָבָהּ יְרוֹפֵף
יַעֲלָה בָּחֲרָה עֲלֵי־עָשׁ מְנוּחָה   5
רַחֲמִי אָת־אֲשֶׁר עֲדֵי־עָשׁ יְעוֹפֵף׃

36

THE GARDEN OF HIS DELIGHT

Cant. 4.16. Let my belovèd come into his garden
Cant. 1,12. And prepare his table and his seat,
To feed in the gardens.

The glorious flowers of the garden of his
delight—
On these shall he set his eyes,
To gather lilies;

Cant. 7,14. And shall eat the hidden fruits,
The new and old.

My belovèd, turn in to me,
To my porch and my temples;
To feed in the gardens

Show thyself in my tents,
Among the beds of mine aloe trees[1].
To gather lilies

Behold, for thee, breasts of pomegranates
Given for a gift!

My belovèd is mine and I am his
When I knock at the habitation of his temple;
To feed in the gardens

[1] My tents אֳהָלִי; my aloes אֲהָלִי

36

גן עדנו

```
א נ) — — — — — — | — — — — — — —
ב ד) — — — — | — — — — —
ה) — — — — — | — — — — — —
```

יָבֹא דוֹדִי לְגַנּוֹ   וְיָכִין מְסִבּוֹ וְכַנּוֹ
לִרְעוֹת בַּגַּנִּים

הוֹד פִּרְחֵי גַן עָדְנוֹ   עֲלֵיהֶם יִתֵּן עֵינוֹ
לִלְקֹט שׁוֹשַׁנִּים

וְיָאֱרֶה מְגָדִים צְפוּנִים   חֲדָשִׁים גַּם יְשָׁנִים:[1]

דוֹדִי סוּרָה אֵלִי   לְאוּלְמִי וְהֵיכָלִי   5
לִרְעוֹת בַּגַּנִּים

הֵרָאָה בְאָהֳלִי   בֵּינוֹת עֲרוּגוֹת אָהֳלִי
לִלְקֹט שׁוֹשַׁנִּים

הֵאָלֵךְ שְׁדַי רִמּוֹנִים   מַתָּנָה נְתוּנִים: 10

לִי דוֹדִי וַאֲנִי לוֹ   בְּדָפְקִי נְוֵה הֵיכָלוֹ
לִרְעוֹת בַּגַּנִּים

[1 Some editions insert after line 5 the following
two lines: כֵּן בְּנֵי שֹׁמְרֵי אֱמָנִים   יְשִׂישׂוּן עוֹד בַּחֲתָנִים
דְּשֵׁנִים וְרַעֲנַנִּים   Ed.]

Cant. 2,4.   His banner over me is love,
Cant. 2,6.   And his left hand is under my head;
                              To gather lilies
                    He waters the gardens with a fountain,
Isa. 33,16.   His waters are faithful.

Ezek. 23,6.   The chosen of desire are met:
                    They disport themselves in the garden of
                         love;
                              To feed in the gardens
Jer. 2,21.   Precious plants they plant,
Isa. 6,13.   Holy seed they sow,
Ezra 9,2.   *To gather lilies*
Isa. 17,10.   Cuttings of glorious trees,
                    Plants of pleasantness.

Num. 24,5.   How goodly are the tents
                   Where the children of nobles meet,
                             To feed in the gardens
                   Sitting under the shadows,
                   In the gardens by the aloes.
                             To gather lilies
                   God shall give them a heritage of joy—
Ps. 127,3.   Children—the heritage of the Lord.

וְעָלַי אַהֲבָה דִּגְלוֹ וְתַחַת לְרֹאשִׁי שְׂמֹאלוֹ
לְלַקֵּט שׁוֹשַׁנִּים

יָרְוָה בְּמַעְיָן גַּנִּים מֵימָיו נֶאֱמָנִים: 15

בְּחוּרֵי חֶמֶד נִפְגְּעוּ בְּגַן אַהֲבָה יִשְׁתַּעְשְׁעוּ
לִרְעוֹת בַּגַּנִּים

נִטְעֵי שׂוֹרֵק יִטָּעוּ וְזֶרַע קֹדֶשׁ יִזְרָעוּ
לְלַקֵּט שׁוֹשַׁנִּים

שָׁתִילֵי הוֹד נִצָּנִים נִטְעֵי נַעֲמָנִים: 20

מַה־יִּטְּבוּ אֹהָלִים שָׁם נִפְגְּעוּ בְּנֵי אֲצִילִים
לִרְעוֹת בַּגַּנִּים

וְשִׁבְתָּם תַּחַת צְלָלִים ¹ כַּגַּנּוֹת עֲלֵי אֳהָלִים
לְלַקֵּט שׁוֹשַׁנִּים

אַל יַנְחִילֵם עֲדָנִים נַחֲלַת אֲדֹנָי בָּנִים: 25

[¹ The translator seems to read בַּנּוֹת, which makes better sense. Ed.].

37

DOVE BESIDE THE WATER BROOKS

Cant. 5,12.   Dove beside the water brooks—
Gen. 3,6.   A delight is she to the eyes.

Job 28,1.   Lo, there is a mine for silver,
              But one like my dove, who can find?
Cant. 6,4.   Beautiful is my love like Tirzah,
                Comely as Jerusalem.

Why turneth she hither and thither
To dwell in tents,
Since in my heart is a camp for her dwelling,
Ps. 104,25.   Great and wide?

Her bosom hath taken spoil of my heart
And wrought upon me
Enchantments, which the magicians
        Of Egypt could not do.

37

יוֹנָה עַל אֲפִיקֵי מִים:

זולת לשבת חתונה

– – – – –

יוֹנָה עַל־אֲפִיקֵי מָיִם
תַּאֲוָה הִיא לָעֵינָיִם:

הֵן יֵשׁ לַכֶּסֶף מוֹצָא
וּכְיוֹנָתִי מִי יִמְצָא
יָפָה רַעְיָתִי כְּתִרְצָה 5
נָאוָה כִּירוּשָׁלָיִם:

וּלְאָנָה וְאָנָה תִפְנֶה
לִשְׁכֹּן בָּאֳהָלִים וְהִנֵּה
בִּלְבָבִי לְשִׁכְנָה מַחֲנֶה
גָּדוֹל וּרְחַב יָדָיִם: 10

דַּדֶּיהָ לְלִבִּי שַׁסּוּ
וַיַּעֲשׂרֻבִי וַיְנַסּוּ
לַהֲטֵיהֶם אֲשֶׁר לֹא יַעֲשׂוּ
כֵּן חַרְטֻמֵּי מִצְרָיִם:

Consider the glory of a precious stone—
How it is red and how it is white;
And marvel to behold upon one stone
   Seven facets.

Zech. 3,9.
Num. 11,7.

Turn for me into honey the gall of adders:
For every man marrieth for substance,
But I give my heart to thee
   A double portion.

I Sam. 1,5.

Cheek of lilies, and mine eyes gathering;
Breasts of pomegranates, and mine hands
    harvesting;
If thy lips be glowing coals
   Then let my jaws be tongs!

Thy two locks of hair are like an ambush
For the wolves of evening;
The light of thy cheek mingleth with them
   Like morning light amid the shadows.

A graceful doe, like gold of Ophir,
With her light she shameth the light of day;
Like the moon, like paved work of sapphire,
   As it were the very heaven.

Ex. 24,10.

הוֹד אָבָן יְקָרָה הַבֵּן 15
אֵיךְ תֵּאָדַם וְאֵיךְ תִּתְלַבֵּן
וּתְמַהּ בַּחֲזוֹת עַל־אָבָן
אַחַת שִׁבְעָה עֵינָיִם:

הָפְכִי־לִי לְצוּף רֹאשׁ פֶּתֶן
כִּי כָל־אִישׁ בְּהוֹן יִתְחַתֵּן 20
וַאֲנִי לָךְ לְבָבִי אֶתֵּן
מָנָה אַחַת אַפָּיִם:

לֶחִי שׁוֹשָׁן וְעֵינַי קְטָפִים
שָׁדֵי רִמּוֹן וְיָדַי אֹסְפִים
אִם שִׂפְתוֹתַיִךְ רְצָפִים 25
מַלְקוֹחַי מָלָקָחַיִם:

וּשְׁתֵּי מַחְלָפוֹת כְּאוֹרֵב
מִשַּׂעֲרֵךְ זְאֵבֵי עָרֶב
אוֹר לֶחְיֵךְ בָּם מִתְעָרֵב
כְּאוֹר בֹּקֶר בֵּין עַרְבָּיִם: 30

יַעֲלַת־חֵן וְכֶתֶם אוֹפִיר
בִּמְאוֹרָהּ מְאוֹר יוֹם תַּחְפִּיר
וּלְבָנָה כְּלִבְנַת סַפִּיר
וּכְעֶצֶם הַשָּׁמָיִם:

There is no darkness before her radiance,
Prov. 31,18. Her lamp is not quenched at night;
To the light of day her light is joined,
Isa. 30,26.   Till it be sevenfold.

This lover hath no friend at his side:
Gen. 2,18. Come thou, be a help for him.
For it is not good that man should be alone,
Eccl. 4,9.   But goodly to be twain.

Ezek. 16,8. The times of love draw nigh to thee,
The season cometh to make us one;
So shall draw near the time of times
Cant. 7,1.   To the dancing of two camps.

חֹשֶׁךְ אֵין לְנֶגֶד זָהֳרָהּ 35
לֹא־יִכְבֶּה בְּלַיְלָה נֵרָהּ
וְעַל־אוֹר יוֹם נוֹסַף אוֹרָהּ
וַיְהְיָה לְשִׁבְעָתָיִם:

זֶה דוֹד וְאֵין רַעְיָה לְצִדּוֹ
בָּאֵי הַיְיָ עֵזֶר כְּנֶגְדּוֹ 40
כִּי לֹא־טוֹב הֱיוֹתוֹ לְבַדּוֹ
וְטוֹבִים הַשְּׁנָיִם:

קָרְבוּ לָךְ עִתּוֹת דּוֹדִים
וּבָא מוֹעֵד לִהְיוֹת אֲחָדִים
כֵּן יְקָרֵב מוֹעֵד מוֹעֲדִים 45
לִמְחֹלַת הַמַּחֲנָיִם:

38

FORSAKEN

(The Hebrew text is translated from an Arabic song)

(For rhymed version see page 161)

I am of little worth and poor when parted
From my glory, and my limbs become like a
    shadow,
Until I am grown old, but not by reason of
    my years.
For lo, my witnesses—the years of my pil-
    grimage!
But I have grown old in his faithlessness;
    for if indeed
He would return to me, my youth too would
    return.

38

לפרוד

העתקה משיר ערבי

‏‐ ‐ | ‐ ‐ ◡ | ‐ ‐ | ‐ ‐ ◡ | ‐ ‐ ◡ | ‐ ‐ ◡ ‐ ▪

נְקַלּוֹתִי וְדַלּוֹתִי לְפֵרוּד

צְבִי וַיְהִיוּ כַצֵּל יְצָרִי

עֲדֵי שַׁבְתִּי וְלֹא מֵרֹב שְׁנוֹתַי

וְהֵן עֲדֵי שְׁנֵי חַיֵּי מְגוּרָי

אֲבָל שַׁבְתִּי בְּבִגְדוֹ־בִי וְאִלּוּ

יְשׁוּבֵנִי יְשׁוּבוּן לִי נְעוּרָי:

5

III. POEMS OF FRIENDSHIP

39

TO RABBI ISAAC THE ORPHAN

Earth, like a little child, was sucking
But yesterday the rains of winter, with a
    cloud for nurse;
Or she was a bride prisoned by the winter,
Whose soul was yearning for the times of love.
She longed for the wooing-time until the
    summer came,
And then the longing heart was healed.

Cant. 5,13. With raiment of golden terraces and broidered
    work of linen, she is like a maid
Delighting, revelling in her fair attire;
Each day she maketh changes in her broideries
And apportioneth apparel unto all about her.
From day to day she changeth the colours of
    her plants
From hue of pearl to sard and emerald.[1]
White is she now and green, and now she is
    red;
She is like a fair one kissing her belovèd.
So beautiful are her flowers that meseemeth
She hath robbed the very stars on high.

[1] For alternative renderings in English of names of
precious stones, see *British Museum* (*Natural History*)
Special Guide (*No 5*) *to Exhibition of Animals, Plants,
and Minerals mentioned in the Bible*, sec. ed. London, 1911.

39

בך הגביר יצחק

‒ ‒ ‿ ‒ | ‒ ‿ ‒ ‒ | ‒ ‿ ‒ ‒ |

אֶרֶץ כְּיַלְדָּה הָיְתָה יוֹנֶקֶת
גִּשְׁמֵי סְתָו אֶתְמוֹל וְעָב מֵינֶקֶת
אוֹ הָיְתָה כַלָּה כְּלוּאָה בַסְּתָו
נַפְשָׁהּ לְעִתּוֹת אַהֲבָה שׁוֹקֶקֶת
חָשְׁקָה לְעֵת דּוֹדִים עֲדֵי נָגַע זְמָן   5
קַיִץ וּבוֹ נִרְפָּא לְבַב חֶשְׁקַת
בִּלְבוּשׁ עֲרוּגַת פָּז וְרִקְמַת שֵׁשׁ כְּבַת
מִתְעַנְּגָה בִּלְבוּשׁ וּמִתְפַּנֶּקֶת
כָּל־יוֹם חֲלִיפוֹת הָרְקָמוֹת תַּחֲלִיף
וּלְכָל־סְבִיבֶיהָ כְּסוּת חֶלְקֶת   10
מִיּוֹם לְיוֹם עֵינֵי צְמָחִים תֵּהָפֵךְ
עֵין דַּר לְעֵין אֹדֶם וְעֵין בָּרֶקֶת
תַּלְבִּין וְתוֹרִיק עֵת וְגַם עֵת תַּאֲדִים
תַּמְשִׁיל צְבָיֶהָ אַהֲבָה נָשֶׁקֶת
יָפוּ פְרָחֶיהָ מְאֹד עַד אָחֲשׁוֹב   15
כִּי כוֹכְבֵי־אֵל הָיְתָה עֹשֶׁקֶת

Cant. 4,13.
Ps. 78,21.
The garden of her plants have we sought early
With the daughter of the vine, that burneth
    with flames of love—
Cold as the cold snow in the hand of him that
    holdeth her,
But within him she is like a kindling fire:
Out of an earthen vessel she riseth like the
    sun;[1]
We bring a cup of onyx and she is poured forth.
With her we walk under the shadows, about
The garden that laugheth through the weeping
    of the showers;
That rejoiceth while the tears of the clouds
    are on her face,
Like a sprinkling of crystals scattered from a
    necklace;
That is glad for the swallow's voice, as for
    sweet wine,[2]

Nahum 2,8.
Ezek. 7,16.
And the voice of the dove cooing and taking
    sweet counsel,
Singing through her leaves as a maiden singeth
Nahum 2,5.
Through her veil, leaping and flitting to and fro.

My soul seeketh eagerly for the morning wind,
For therein it embraceth the perfume of the
    belovèd—
The wind that playeth with the myrtle to
    make it waft
Its perfume to them that love, but are very
    far away.

[1] חֶרֶשׂ "earthen" and חֶרֶס "the sun" are identical in sound

[2] This for the sake of the similarity in sound in the words עֲסִיס and תָּשִׂישׂ סִיס

פַּרְדֵּס שְׁלָחָיהָ שֶׁחַרְנוּהוּ בְּבַת־

נָפֶן בְּרִשְׁפֵּי אַהֲבָה נִשָּׁקֶת

קָרָה כְּקֹר שֶׁלֶג בְּיַד תִּפְשָׂהּ אֲבָל

בֵּינוֹת קְרָבָיו הִיא כְּאֵשׁ דּוֹלָקֶת   20

מִתּוֹךְ כְּלִי חָרָשׂ כְּחָרָס תַּעֲלֶה

נַגִּישׁ כְּלִי שֶׁהֵם וְהִיא מוּצָקֶת

בָּהּ נִהֲלֵךְ תַּחַת צְלָלִים עַל־סָבִיב

גַּנָּה לְבִכְיַת הֶרְבִיב שֹׂחָקֶת

תִּשְׂמַח וְדִמְעַת עָב בְּפָנֶיהָ רְסִיס   25

כְּזֹרֵק בְּדֹלַח מֵעֲנָק זָרָקֶת

תָּשִׁישׁ עֲלֵי קוֹל סִיס כְּעַל עָסִיס וְקוֹל

יוֹנָה מְנַהֶגֶת וְסוֹד מַמְתָּקֶת

תָּרָן בְּעַד עָלֶה כְּרָן עַלְמָה בְּעַד

מָסָךְ וְרֹקֶדֶת וּמִשְׁתַּקְשָׁקֶת   30

נַפְשִׁי לְרוּחַ הַשְּׁחָרִים שֶׁחֲרָה

כִּי בָהּ לְרֵיחַ הַיָּדִיד חֹבָקֶת

רוּחַ מְשַׂחֶקֶת וְתָנִיף הַהֲדַס

רֵיחוֹ לְחֹשְׁקִים רָחֲקוּ מַרְחָקֶת

And the myrtle boughs rise proudly aloft and
    bend low,

And the palm branches clap their hands at
    the singing of the birds,

Waving and bowing before the face

Of Isaac, and the whole world laughing with
    his name,

Gen. 21,6.   For she said, "Hath not God made me to
    laugh

Since I take fast hold of the cords of Isaac?"

I speak, and none denieth my words, in praise

Of his honour; and every ear that hearkeneth
    consenteth.

The fame of all princes is divided between
    good and evil,

Yet surely is his name only good without
    dissent.

How sweet to mine ear to hear of him
While my soul is busied in remembering him;
Aye, beholding his likeness, it addeth the more—

Prov. 25,1.   Even twofold praise, re-echoing the song.
Of thee, O lordly Isaac, my tongue shall sing

Isa. 32,4.   Glowing words, flowing songs without pause;

For I make a covenant with thee, for the days
    of my life,

That my tongue shall not be silent from thy
    praise.

Which shall I set first of thy praises,
Since thy soul is joined to every honour?

With thee do noble thoughts pitch their
    tents;

וּסְעִיף הֲדַס יִגְאֶה וְיִכָּפֵל וְכַף 35

תָּמָר בְּרָן צִפּוֹר לְכַף סִפָּקֶת

מִתְנוֹפְפָה מִשְׁתַּחֲוָה נֶגֶד פְּנֵי

יִצְחָק וְתֵבֵל עִם־שְׁמוֹ צֹחָקֶת

תֹאמַר הֲלֹא עָשָׂה אֱלֹהִים לִי צְחוֹק

כִּי בַעֲבֻת יִצְחָק אֲנִי מַחֲזֶקֶת 40

אָמַר וְאֵין מֵשִׁיב אֲמָרַי עַל־שְׁבַח

הוֹדוֹ וְאֹזֶן שֶׁמְעָה מִצִּדְקָת

שֵׁם כָּל־נְדִיבִים נֶחֱלַק אֶל־טוֹב וָרָע

אָכֵן שְׁמוֹ רַק טוֹב בְּלִי מַחְלָקֶת

מַה־נֶּעֱמָה אָזְנִי בְּשָׁמְעוֹ כַּאֲשֶׁר 45

נַפְשִׁי בְּזִכְרוֹ הָיְתָה עוֹסָקֶת

אַךְ בַּחֲזוֹתָהּ אֶת־דְּמוּתוֹ יָסְפָה

שֶׁבַח וְכִפְלַיִם לְשִׁיר מַעְתָּקֶת

בָּךְ הַגְּבִיר יִצְחָק לְשׁוֹנִי תַעֲנֶה

צָחוֹת וְשִׁיר תַּחְבִּיר וְלֹא־מַפְסָקֶת 50

כִּי אָכְרְתָה עִמָּךְ יְמֵי חַיַּי בְּרִית

מִמַּהֲלָלְךָ בַּל־תֶּהִי שֹׁתָקֶת

מַה־זֹּאת אֲקַדֵּם מִשְׁבָחֶיךָ וְהֵן

נַפְשָׁךְ בְּכָל־מִינֵי יְקָר מְדֻבָּקֶת

בָּךְ הַנְּדִיבוֹת אָהֳלֵיהֶם תָּקָעוּ 55

Jud. 4,10. Unto thee understanding calleth a camp
     together.
Prov. 7,18. Thy soul hath taken her fill of the love of
     knowledge
  And penetrateth unto the last secret;
Ps. 84,4. For she hath found her a nest in thy heart,
  Delighting herself in thee and leaning upon thee.
  Therefore be fruitful and multiply and give
     as heritage to thy seed
  The spirit of nobleness which is thine and the
     liberal hand;
  And see children's children unto thy children,
     and may a cloud
  Be pouring forth mercy upon them.

וּלֵךְ תְּבוּנָה מַחֲנֵה מַזְעָקַת

נַפְשְׁךָ בְּדוֹדֵי הַתְּבוּנָה רֵוְתָה

וּלְתַעֲלֻמָה אַחֲרִית בּוֹדָקַת

כִּי מֶצְאָה קֵן לָהּ בְּלִבָּךְ וַתְּהִי

מִשְׁתַּעְשְׁעָה עִמָּךְ וּמִתְרַפָּקַת

לָכֵן פְּרֵה וּרְבֵה וְהַנְחֵל זַרְעֲךָ

רוּחַ נְדִיבָה לָךְ וְיָד מַעֲנָקֶת

וּרְאֵה בְּנֵי בָנִים לְבָנֶיךָ וְעָב

חָסֶד עֲלֵיהֶם תִּהְיֶה יוֹצָקַת:

60

40

TO RABBI SAMUEL HA-NAGID

Nahum 3,17. The chosen of crowns
   For the chosen of crowned,
 And the song of songs
   For the prince of princes!

 Set thou a watchman;
Isa. 21,6.   What he seeth let him tell:
 He will see the chariot
   Of Samuel the Prince;
Ex. 15,20. And timbrels and dances
   Ranged round about him;
 For every neck a chain
Ezek. 16,11. And on every hand a bracelet;
 He goeth out in his thousands,
Num. 9,16. And so may he ever be—

 To rescue the martyrs,
  To loose the bound.

 Thou art fairer
Ps. 45,3.   Than the sons of men—
 So art thou worthy
   To be their prince.
 Thy shadow is a canopy
Isa. 4,5.   Over all their glory,
Jer. 29,7. Their peace is in thy peace,
   And of thine honour is their honour;
 In thy shadow they live
   Among a nation that enslaveth them,

40

שמואל הנגיד

‒ ‒ ‒ ‒ ‒ | ‒ ‒ ‒ ‒

לְמִבְחַר מְנָזָרִים	מִבְחַר נְזָרִים
לְשַׂר הַשָּׂרִים:	וְשִׁיר הַשִּׁירִים

אֲשֶׁר יִרְאֶה יַגִּיד	הַעֲמֵד הַמִּצְפֶּה
שְׁמוּאֵל הַנָּגִיד	וְרָאָה מִרְכָּבֶת
אֲשֶׁר סְבִיבָיו הֶעֱמִיד	וְתֻפִּים וּמְחֹלוֹת 5
וְעַל־כָּל־יָד צָמִיד	לְכָל־צַוָּאר רָבִיד
וְכֵן יִהְיֶה תָמִיד	יָצָא בַאֲלָפָיו

וְהַתֵּר נֶאֱסָרִים:	לְהַצִּיל נִמְסָרִים

מִבְּנֵי אָדָם	יָפְיָפִיתָ
לִהְיוֹת נְגִידָם	וְכֵן זָכִיתָ 10
עַל־כָּל־כְּבוֹדָם	וְצִלְּךָ חָפָּה
וּמֵהוֹדְךָ הוֹדָם	שְׁלוֹמָם בִּשְׁלוֹמֶךָ
עִם־גּוֹיֵ מַעֲבִידָם	בְּצִלְּךָ יִחְיוּ

Cant. 2.2. Like lilies abiding
    In the midst of thorns.

II Kings 2,11– He is a chariot for his people
12.   And he their horseman,
Prov. 15,4. And a tree of life and healing,
Ezek. 47,12.   Bringing forth new fruit every month,
    By the rivers of righteousness
Jer. 17,8.   Spreading out his roots
I Kings 10.8. Happy are his servants,
II Chron. 9,7.   And happy are his men;
    He ruleth yet with God
Hosea 12,1.   And is faithful among His saints.

And his works are brought to remembrance
    To teach uprightness.

The heart of the proud ones of Shinar[1]
    Cry out to behold him,
And the councillors of Egypt
    Yearn after his mouth;
For his thoughts
    In God's secret counsel are shining,
When a man inquireth
II Sam. 16,23.   Of the word of God.
He is a refuge and a strength
    To those trembling and astounded

In dens of young lions,
Cant. 4.8.   On mountains of leopards.

Unto the uttermost part of the earth,
    Take wing,[2] O my songs!

    [1] Babylon.
    [2] Reading כְּנָף "wing". Another reading is כַּף "hand".

בֵּין הַדַּרְדָּרִים: כְּשׁוֹשַׁנִּים דָּרִים

וְהוּא פָרָשָׁיו   הוּא לְעַמּוֹ רָכָב   15

יְבַכֵּר לַחֲדָשָׁיו   וְעֵץ חַיִּים מַרְפֵּא

יְשַׁלַּח שָׁרָשָׁיו   עַל פְּלָנֵי־צֶדֶק

וְאַשְׁרֵי אֲנָשָׁיו   אַשְׁרֵי עֲבָדָיו

וְנֶאֱמָן עִם קְדוֹשָׁיו   עוֹד רָד עִם־אֵל

לְלַמֵּד מֵישָׁרִים: 20 וּמַעֲשָׂיו נִזְכָּרִים

לַחֲזוֹתוֹ יָהִים   לֵב גְּאוֹנֵי שִׁנְעָר

אַחֲרֵי פִיו נִגְהִים   וְיוֹעֲצֵי מִצְרַיִם

בְּסוֹד אֵל נִגְהִים   כִּי מַחֲשָׁבָיו

בִּדְבַר הָאֱלֹהִים   כַּאֲשֶׁר יִשְׁאַל־אִישׁ

חֲרֵדִים וּתְמֵהִים   מַחֲסָה וָעֹז לַ־   25

וְהָרֵי הַנְּמֵרִים: בִּמְעוֹנוֹת כְּפִירִים

שְׂאוּ כָנָף, רַנֵּנִי!   אֶל־כְּנַף הָאָרֶץ

Publish tidings in Spain
  To my brethren and my sons,
That I minister
  Unto Samuel, the chief of my princes,
And Samuel doth minister

I Sam. 2,18.   Before the face of the Lord;
And I had not believed to see
  That which mine eyes have beheld—

Prov. 12,18. A tongue of healing for bodies,
  And life for the flesh.

וּבַשְׂרוּ בִסְפָרַד　　לְאַחַי וּבָנַי

כִּי אֲנִי מְשָׁרַת　　שְׁמוּאֵל רֹאשׁ קְצִינַי

וּשְׁמוּאֵל מְשָׁרַת　　אֶת־פְּנֵי יְיָ　　30

וְלֹא־הֶאֱמַנְתִּי רְאוֹת　　אֲשֶׁר רָאוּ עֵינַי

לְשׁוֹן מַרְפֵּא פְנָרִים　　וְחַיֵּי בְשָׂרִים:

41

TO RABBI MOSES IBN EZRA—
ON PARTING

We know thee, O separation, from the days of
    youth,

Jud. 5,21. And the river of weeping—that ancient river!
Shall we strive with fate, that hath not sinned,
And with days, though days bear no iniquity?
They run in circles, in a right course,
And naught is perverse nor crooked in the
    Heights.—

Can this be a new thing, since naught in the
    world is new,

And since her laws are inscribed by the
    finger of God?

And how shall her words change, since they
    all

Ps. 77,11. Are sealed by the ring on the right hand of
    the Most High?

And every cause is re-found in the circuit,

And every new thing hath been already many
    times;

And man is united but to be parted again,

Gen. 25,23. To bring forth out of one nation many nations.

Gen. 11,1-9. For had not the sons of man been divided
    from of old,

Then would the earth not be filled with peoples.

41

לנד משה

‖ ‒ ‒ ⏑ ‒ | ‒ ‒ ‒ | ‒ ‒ ⏑

יְדַעְנוּךָ נְדֹד מִימֵי עֲלוּמִים
וְנַחַל הַבְּכִי נַחַל קְדוּמִים
הֲרֹב עִם הַזְּמָן עַל־לֹא חֲטָאָה
וְעִם־יָמִים וְאֵין עָוֹן לְיָמִים
פְּלָכִים הֵם בְּקַר־צֶדֶק יְרוּצוּן   5
וְאֵין נִפְתָּל וְעִקֵּשׁ בַּמְּרוֹמִים
הֲזֶה חָדָשׁ וְאֵין תֵּבֵל חֲדָשָׁה
וְחֻקֶּיהָ בְּאֶצְבַּע אֵל רְשׁוּמִים
וְאֵיךְ יִשְׁנוּ דְבָרֶיהָ וְכֻלָּם
בְּטַבַּעַת יְמִין עֶלְיוֹן חֲתוּמִים   10
וְכָל־סִבָּה מְצוּאָה בַּמְּסִבָּה
וְכָל־חָדָשׁ כְּבָר הָיָה פְעָמִים
וְלֹא חֻבַּר אֱנוֹשׁ כִּי אִם־לְפָרֵד
לְהוֹצִיא מִלְאֹם אֶחָד לְאֻמִּים
וְלוּלֵא נִפְרְדוּ מֵאָז בְּנֵי־אִישׁ   15
אֲזַי לֹא־מָלְאָה אֶרֶץ עֲמָמִים

A thing may be which is both good and evil,

Prov. 3,8; 14,30. That hath in it both marrow and rottenness
    for the bones:

Isa. 8,21. If a man wax wrathful he curseth his day,
And denounceth his angered moments;
Yet that is the day that others bless,

Job 21,13. The very day they spend in pleasantness.
Moreover, all food in the mouth of the healthy
    man is like honey,
But honey in the mouth of the sick is like
    juniper.[1]
And as for him that sorroweth, the lights are
    dark to his eyes:
He seeth them not—they are hidden from him—

Ex. 40,35. Like mine eyes, on this day when the cloud
    resteth upon them,
When they pour forth floods at the parting
    from Moses—
The fount of wisdom, in whose mouth I find
The place of gold, the mine of purest ore.

Friendship bound up my soul with his soul
While the chariots of flight were not yet
    harnessed,
While as yet my soul had not adventured upon
    parting,
And the sons of the days were all with us
    complete.
The daughters of the days did bear us singly,
But the daughter of love bore us as twins,

Cant. 5,13. In faithfulness, upon a bed of spices,

---

[1] Compare Marcus Aurelius: VI, lii.

וְיֵשׁ דָּבָר אֲשֶׁר יֵיטַב וְיֵרַע

וּבוֹ שִׁקּוּי וְרָקָב לָעֲצָמִים

בְּהִתְקַצֵּף אֱנוֹשׁ יוֹמוֹ יְקַלֵּל 20

וְיִקֹּב אֶת־דְּרָגָעָיו הַזְּעוּמִים

וְהוּא הַיּוֹם יְבָרְכוּהוּ אֲחֵרִים

אֲשֶׁר אֹתוֹ יְבַלּוּ בַנְּעִימִים

וְכָל־מַאֲכָל בְּפִי בָרִיא כְּנֹפֶת

וְהַנֹּפֶת בְּפִי חֹלֶה רְתָמִים

וְדֹאֵג יַחְשְׁכוּ אוֹרִים בְּעֵינָיו 25

וְלֹא יִרְאַם וְהֵם לוֹ נֶעֱלָמִים

כְּעֵינֵי יוֹם שָׁכַן עָנָן עֲלֵיהֶם

לְנֹד מֹשֶׁה וְהֵם יָרְדוֹת זְרָמִים

מְקוֹר חָכְמָה אֲשֶׁר אָמְצָא בְּפִיהוּ

מְקוֹם הַפָּז וּמַחֲצַב הַכְּתָמִים 30

יְדִידוּת קֻשְּׁרָה נַפְשִׁי בְּנַפְשׁוֹ

בְּעוֹד רִכְבֵי נְדֹד אֵינָם רְתוּמִים

בְּעוֹד לֹא נִסְּתָה נַפְשִׁי פְּרִידָה

וְאִתָּנוּ בְּנֵי יָמִים שְׁלֵמִים

יְלָדוּנוּ בְנוֹת יָמִים פְּרֻדִים 35

וּבַת־אַהֲבָה יְלָדַתְנוּ תְאוֹמִים

אֱמָנִים עַל־עֲרוּגַת הַבְּשָׂמִים

Isa. 66,11.

Sucking the breasts of the daughter of the
        vineyards.
I remember thee upon the Mountains of
        Separation
Which were but yesterday, through thy
        presence, the Mountains of Spices,[1]
And mine eyelids are tarnished with tears,

Isa. 9,4.

And the tears defiled with blood.

I remember thee, and am remembered, in the
        days
That we passed, and they were like dreams.

Time, the deceiver of all men, hath given me in
        exchange for thee

Jer. 9,7;
Ps. 55,22.

Such as have war in their heart and peace in
        their mouth.
I speak with them, even though I find within
        their mouth,

Num. 11,5.

In lieu of thy manna, leeks and garlic.
My rage and my wrath is upon those foolish
        ones

Isa. 5,21.

Who are wise in their own eyes,
Who call their falsenesses faiths,
And call my faith superstition;
Who sow and reap their ears of corn
And rejoice in them even though they be
        blasted.
The exterior of knowledge is as earthenware[2]

[1] Compare Cant. 2,17 הָרֵי בָתֶר and 8,14 הָרֵי בְשָׂמִים.

[2] Brody had read this obscure passage וְצַוַּנִי דְּבַר חָכְמָה חֲדָשִׁים.

See, however, his subsequent illuminating note to the
Hebrew text No. 41, line 55, which I have now followed.

וַיֹּנִקֵי שֹׁד שָׁדַי בַּת הַכְּרָמִים

זְכַרְתִּיךְ עֲלֵי הָרֵי בְתָרִים

תְּמוֹל הָיוּ בָךְ הָרֵי בְשָׂמִים 40

וְעַפְעַפַּי מְגוֹלָלִים בְּדִמְעָה

וְהַדִּמְעָה מְגוֹלָלָה בְדָמִים

זְכַרְתִּיךְ וְנִזְכַּרְתִּי לְיָמִים

עֲבָרְנוּמוֹ וְהָיוּ כַחֲלֹמִים

הֲמִירְךָ לִי זְמָן בֶּגֶד בְּכָל-אִישׁ 45

אֲשֶׁר לִבּוֹ קְרָב וּבְפִיו שְׁלוֹמִים

אֲדַבֵּר-בָּם וְאִם אֶמְצָא בְפִיהֶם

תְּמוּרַת מַנְךָ חָצִיר וְשׁוּמִים

חֲמָסִי וַחֲמָתִי עַל-פְּתָאִים

אֲשֶׁר הֵמָּה בְעֵינֵיהֶם חֲכָמִים 50

אֲשֶׁר קָרְאוּ לְשִׁקְרֵיהֶם אֱמוּנוֹת

וְקָרְאוּ שֵׁם אֱמוּנָתִי קְסָמִים

אֲשֶׁר זָרְעוּ וְקָצְרוּ שַׁבְּלֵיהֶם

וְשָׂמְחוּ בָם וְאִם הֵמָּה צְנֻמִים

וְחִיצוֹנַי דְּבַר חָכְמָה חֲרָשִׁים 55

To cover up the innermost pearls;
But torches are mine wherewith to search
    his chambers,
And to bring forth from his hidden treasuries
    the gems.[1]
And I cannot rest until the sheaves

Bow down in wisdom to my sheaf.
And when a fool seeketh the secret, I answer
    him:

What hath a ring of gold to do upon a swine's
    snout?
And how, upon a sterile place, should I seek
For my clouds to drop their rains?
And my need from fortune is light and pass-
    ing,
Like the need of the soul for the body,
Which, in so far as it holdeth her she giveth
    it life,
But when it wearieth she abandoneth it like
    an effigy.

---

[1] The wisdom of his friend.

לְכַסּוֹת הַפְּנִינִים הַפְּנִימִים
וְלִי נֵרוֹת אֲחַפֵּשׂ־בָּם חֲדָרָיו
וְאוֹצִיא מִגְּנָזָיו הַלְּשָׁמִים
וְלֹא־אֶשְׁקֹט עֲדֵי תִשְׁתַּחֲוֶין,
בְּחָכְמָה לַאֲלָמָתִי אֲלָמִּים   60
וְסָכָל כִּי יְבַקֵּשׁ־סוֹד עֲנִיתִיו
עֲלֵי אַף הַחֲזִיר מַה־לַּנְּזָמִים
וְאֵיךְ עֲל־לֹא מְקוֹם זֶרַע אֲבַקֵּשׁ
עֲנֵנִי לַעֲרֹף עָלָיו גְּשָׁמִים
וְצָרְכִּי לַזְּמָן נָקֵל וְנִדְמָה   65
כְּמוֹ־צָרְךָ נְשָׁמָה לַגְּשָׁמִים
אֲשֶׁר מִדֵּי יְכִילוּהָ תְּחַיֵּם
וְאִם־יִכְלָאוּ עֲזָבְתַם צְלָמִים:

42

THE PASSING OF RABBI BARUCH[1]

Joel 1,14; 2,15. Why do the people call a solemn assembly?
Let them alone, for bitter
II Kings 4,27. Is the soul of all the people.

The Law is perished from Sinai,
And they thirst for the word of the Lord,
Ex. 17,1. But there is no water to give drink to the
people.

Ex. 9,3. Lo, the hand of the Lord hath been
Against the great mountain that was
I Sam. 9,2. High over all the people.

The sun and the moon have gone down,
And heavy cloud is upon the mountain,
Ex. 19,16. And trembling seizeth all the people.

The destroying angel hath set his face,
Ezek. 10,2. Hath filled his arms with coals of fire,
Ex. 24,8. And hath sprinkled them on the people.

I moan and cry in my burning fire,
I say unto Fate in the bitterness of my soul:
Ex. 5,22. Why hast thou dealt ill with this people?

Job 16,7. Lo, all mine assembly thou madest desolate
The day thou didst raise to the skies
Ps. 89,20. One chosen of the people.

[1] According to Harkavy, Rabbi Baruch ben Isaac ben
Baruch Albalia. See *Jewish Encyclopedia* I, p. 321.

42

הרב ברוך

‎— — — — — | — —

מַה־לָעָם יִקְרְאוּ עֲצָרָה   הַרְפֵּה־לָהֶם כִּי־מָרָה
נֶפֶשׁ כָּל־הָעָם:

אָבְדָה תוֹרָה מִסִּינַי   וַיִּצְמְאוּ לִדְבַר אֲדֹנָי
וְאֵין מַיִם לִשְׁתּוֹת הָעָם:

הִנֵּה יַד־אֲדֹנָי הוֹיָה   בָּהָר־הַגָּדוֹל אֲשֶׁר הָיָה
גָּבֹהַ מִכָּל־הָעָם:

בָּאוּ שֶׁמֶשׁ וְהַסַּהַר   וְעָנָן כָּבֵד עַל־הָהָר
וַיֶּחֱרַד כָּל־הָעָם:

מַלְאָךְ מַשְׁחִית שָׁם פָּנָיו   וּמִלֵּא בִרְשָׁפֵי אֵשׁ הָפָנָיו
וַיִּזְרֹק עַל־הָעָם:

אֶדְאַג וְאֶשְׁאַג בְּדֹם אִשִּׁי   וְאֹמַר לַזְּמָן בְּמַר נַפְשִׁי
לָמָה הֲרֵעֹתָה לָעָם:

הֵן כָּל־עֲדָתִי הֲשַׁמּוֹתָ   יוֹם לַשַּׂחֵק הֲרִימוֹתָ
בָּחוּר מֵעָם:

Cease, for thou workest sore destruction
When thou takest a sword to slay
Jud. 20,2.   The chiefs of all the people.

The cloud hath departed from them,
And the manna hath not come down for them,
Num. 21,4.   And crushed is the soul of the people.

Inheriting and bequeathing the law of the
    Judges
From the seed of the Princes
Jud. 5,9.   Who gave themselves willingly among the
    people,

His words shone like the light,
And his ways were exceeding high
Isa. 8,11.   So that he could not walk in the way of
    the people.

II Kings 12,13. Standing to repair the breach,
Prov. 20,8. And sitting on a throne of righteousness
Ex. 18,13.   To judge the people—

Life was the fruit of his law;
Therefore to bear his departure
Ex. 19,23.   Is too hard for the people.

While yet the Chief, Baruch,
Was prepared to battle for me,
Ps. 3,7.   I feared not from tens of thousands of
    people.

Isa. 57,15.   Meek, lowly of spirit and humble,
The wisdom of his gentle tongue
Ps. 18,44.   Would deliver me from the strivings of
    the people.

15 הָרָף כִּי מְאֹד הֻשְׁחַתְּ   בְּקַחְתְּךָ חֶרֶב וְהַמַּטֶּה
פְּנוֹת כָּל־הָעָם:

עָנָן מֵעֲלֵיהֶם נִפְרָד   וְהַמָּן עֲלֵיהֶם לֹא־יֵרַד
וַתִּקְצַר נֶפֶשׁ הָעָם:

נֹחַל וּמַנְחִיל דָּת פְּלִילִים   מִזֶּרַע הָאֲצִילִים
הַמִּתְנַדְּבִים בָּעָם: 20

מְלָיו כְּאוֹר נֶנְהוּ   וּדְרָכָיו מְאֹד גָּבְהוּ
מָלָכְתָּ בְּדֶרֶךְ הָעָם:

עָמַד לְחַזֵּק הַבֶּדֶק   וְיֵשֵׁב עַל־כִּסֵּא צֶדֶק
לִשְׁפֹּט אֶת־הָעָם:

25 חַיִּים הָיָה פְּרִי דָתוֹ   וְעַל־כֵּן לָשֵׂאת פְּרִידָתוֹ
לֹא־יוּכַל הָעָם:

בְּעוֹד הָיָה הָרַב בָּרוּךְ   לְהִלָּחֶם בַּעֲדִי עָרוּךְ
לֹא־אִירָא מֵרִבְבוֹת עָם:

עָנָן שְׁפַל־רוּחַ וְדַכָּא   חָכְמַת לְשׁוֹנוֹ הָרַכָּה
תְּפַלְּטֵנִי מֵרִיבֵי עָם: 30

In the day of battle he would strive for me,
And on the day of prayer he would bring nigh
Levit. 9,15.   The offering of the people.

The balm and the charm have perished,
Jer. 8,17.   And many are the poisonous serpents
Num. 21,6.   Which bite the people.

His land was like a garden of God,
And now that his lofty branches have fallen,
Isa. 40,7.   Surely but grass is the people.

A fount of wisdom ever growing stronger;
Job 33,14.   And trusty—for once he had spoken
Ex. 4,31.   He was believed of the people.

How sweet were the beauteous words
Jer. 36,13.   When Baruch read in the Book
In the ears of the people!

Ps. 80,2.   Guiding with faithfulness, and shepherding,
Seeking those cast out and astray,
Ex. 8,25.   So as not to send away the people;

A fountain of justice, and its lord,
Interpreter of truth, and its tongue,
Neh. 8, 7.   Making it clear to the people;

A good interpreter, telling of uprightness,
He, by his righteousness, made atonement
Levit. 16,24.   For himself and for his people.

In peace he shall place in his stead
And appoint after him his two sons,
Deut. 20,9.   Captains of hosts at the head of the people:

יוֹם קְרָב הוּא בַּעֲדֵי יָרִיב וּבְיוֹם תְּפִלָּה הוּא יַקְרִיב
אֶת קָרְבַּן הָעָם:

אָבַד הַצְּרִי וְהַלָּחַשׁ וְרַבּוּ צִפְעֹנֵי נָחָשׁ
וַיִּנָּשְׁכוּ אֶת־הָעָם:

35 הָיְתָה אַרְצוֹ כְּגַן אֱלֹהִים וּבִנְפֹל סָעִפָּיו הַגְּבֹהִים
אָכֵן חָצִיר הָעָם:

מַעְיַן חָכְמָה מִתְגַּבֵּר וְנֶאֱמָן כִּי בְּאַחַת יְדַבֵּר
וַיַּאֲמֵן הָעָם:

מַה־נָּעֲמוּ אִמְרֵי־שָׁפָר בִּקְרֹא בָרוּךְ בַּסֵּפֶר
בְּאָזְנֵי הָעָם: 40

נֹהַג בָּאֱמוּנָה וְרֹעֶה מְבַקֵּשׁ נִדָּח וְתֹעֶה
לְבִלְתִּי שַׁלַּח אֶת־הָעָם:

מַעְיַן הַדִּין וַאֲדוֹנוֹ יָמְלִיץ יֹשֶׁר וּלְשׁוֹנוֹ
מְבִינִים אֶת־הָעָם:

45 מֵלִיץ טוֹב יָשְׁרוֹ יְסַפֵּר וּבְצִדְקָתוֹ יְכַפֵּר
בַּעֲדוֹ וּבְעַד הָעָם:

בְּשָׁלוֹם יְקַדֵּם אֶת־פָּנָיו וְיִפְקֹד אַחֲרָיו שְׁנֵי בָנָיו
שָׂרֵי צְבָאוֹת בְּרֹאשׁ הָעָם:

A precious son whom God shall instruct,
And a child of delight, his second one—
Gen. 48,19.   He also shall become a people.

Ezek. 37,16.   And all the house of Israel shall be their
                    companions;
            In their days shall the mountains bear
Ps. 72,3.   Peace for the people.

בֶּן יַקִּיר אֵל יְבוֹנְנֵהוּ   וּבֶן שַׁעֲשׁוּעִים מְשָׁנַּהוּ
גַּם הוּא יִהְיֶה־לְעָם: 50

וְכָל־בֵּית יִשְׂרָאֵל חֲבֵרִים   בִּימֵיהֶם יִשְׂאוּ הָרִים
שָׁלוֹם לָעָם:

IV. DEVOTIONAL POEMS

43

BEFORE THEE IS MY WHOLE DESIRE

O Lord, before Thee is my whole desire—
Yea, though I cannot bring it to my lips.

Thy favour I would ask a moment and then
    die—
Ah, would that mine entreaty might be granted!

That I might render up the remnant of my
    spirit to Thine hand,
Then should I sleep, and sweet my sleep
    would be.

When far from Thee, I die while yet in life;
But if I cling to Thee I live, though I should
    die.

Only I know not how to come before Thee,
Nor what should be my service nor my law.

Show me, O Lord, Thy ways!
And turn me back from bondage of my folly;

And teach me, while there yet is power in me
To bear affliction; scorn not mine abasement

Ere yet the day I grow a burden on myself,
The day my limbs weigh heavy each on each;

43

אדני נגדך כל תאותי
בקשה

‒ ⏑ ‒ | ‒ ⏑ ‒ | ‒ ⏑ ‒ ‒ | ⏑ ‒ ‒ ּ

אֲדֹנָי נֶגְדְּךָ כָל־תַּאֲוָתִי

וְאִם־לֹא אַעֲלֶנָּה עַל־שְׂפָתִי

רְצוֹנְךָ אֶשְׁאֲלָה רֶגַע וְאֶגְוָע

וּמִי־יִתֵּן וְתָבוֹא שֶׁאֱלָתִי

וְאַפְקִיד אֶת־שְׁאָר רוּחִי בְּיָדֶךָ   5

וְיָשַׁנְתִּי וְעָרְבָה־לִּי שְׁנָתִי

בְּרָחְקִי מִמְּךָ מוֹתִי בְחַיָּי

וְאִם־אֶדְבַּק בְּךָ חַיַּי בְּמוֹתִי

אֲבָל לֹא־אֵדְעָה בַּמֶּה אֲקַדֵּם

וּמַה־תִּהְיֶה עֲבֹדָתִי וְדָתִי   10

דְּרָכֶיךָ אֲדֹנָי לַמְּדֵנִי

וְשׁוּב מִמַּאֲסַר סִכְלוּת שְׁבוּתִי

וְהוֹרֵנִי בְּעוֹד יֶשׁ־בִּי יְכֹלֶת

לְהִתְעַנּוֹת וְאַל־תִּבְזֶה עֱנוּתִי

בְּטֶרֶם יוֹם אֱהִי עָלַי לְמַשָּׂא   15

וְיוֹם יִכְבַּד קְצָתִי עַל־קְצָתִי

When I am bowed despite me, and the moth
Eateth my bones aweary of sustaining me;

And I fare forth whither my fathers fared,
And where they rested find my camping place.

Stranger and sojourner am I on face of earth,
While in her womb is mine appointed home.

My youth, until to-day, hath done its
　　　pleasure:
But when shall I do good for mine own soul?

Eccl. 3,11.　The world which Thou hast set within my
　　　heart
Hath held me back from seeking out mine
　　　end;

And how then shall I serve my Maker, while
A captive to my lust, a slave to my desire?

And how shall I aspire to lofty place?—
Tomorrow morn the worm will be my sister;

And how upon a day of gladness shall my
　　　heart be glad?—
I know not if it shall be well with my to-
　　　morrow;

For lo, the days and nights are pledged to-
　　　gether
All to consume my flesh till I am gone,

To scatter to the wind the half of me,
And half of me restore unto the dust.

וְאֶכָּנַע בְּעַל־כָּרְחִי וְיֹאכַל

עֲצָמַי עָשׁ וְתִלְאוּ מַשָּׂאתִי

וְאֶסַּע אֶל־מָקוֹם נָסְעוּ אֲבוֹתַי

וּבִמְקוֹם תַּחֲנָתָם תַּחֲנֹתִי 20

כְּגֵר תּוֹשָׁב אֲנִי עַל־גַּב אֲדָמָה

וְאוּלָם כִּי בְּבִטְנָהּ נַחֲלָתִי

נְעוּרַי עַד־הֲלוֹם עָשׂוּ לְנַפְשָׁם

וּמָתַי גַּם־אֲנִי אֶעֱשֶׂה לְבֵיתִי

וְהָעוֹלָם אֲשֶׁר נָתַן בְּלִבִּי 25

מְנָעַנִי לְבַקֵּשׁ אַחֲרִיתִי

וְאֵיכָה אֶעֱבֹד יֹצְרִי בְּעוֹדִי

אֲסִיר יִצְרִי וְעֶבֶד תַּאֲוָתִי

וְאֵיכָה מַעֲלָה רָמָה אֲבַקֵּשׁ

וּמָחָר תִּהְיֶה רִמָּה אֲחוֹתִי 30

וְאֵיךְ יִיטַב בְּיוֹם טוֹבָה לְבָבִי

וְלֹא אֵדַע הֲיִיטַב מָחֳרָתִי

וְהַיָּמִים וְהַלֵּילוֹת עֲרֵבִים

לְכַלּוֹת אֶת־שְׁאָרִי עַד־כְּלוֹתִי

וְלָרוּחַ יְזָרוּן מַחֲצִיתִי 35

וְלֶעָפָר יְשִׁיבוּן מַחֲצִיתִי

What can I say?   Temptation doth pursue me
As doth an enemy, from youth to age;

And what hath fate for me if not Thy favour?
If Thou art not my lot, what is my lot?

I am despoiled and naked of good works,
Thy righteousness alone my covering—

But why make longer speech, why question
          more?
O Lord, before Thee is my whole desire.

וּמָה אֹמַר וְיִצְרִי יִרְדְּפֵנִי
כְּאוֹיֵב מִנְּעוּרַי עַד־בְּלוֹתִי
וּמַה־לִּי בַּזְּמָן אִם לֹא־רְצוֹנֶךָ
וְאִם אֵינֶךָ מְנָתִי מַה־מְּנָתִי

40

אֲנִי מִמַּעֲשִׂים שׁוֹלָל וְעָרוֹם
וְצִדְקָתְךָ לְבַדָּהּ הִיא כְסוּתִי
וְעוֹד מָה אַאֲרִיךְ לָשׁוֹן וְאֶשְׁאַל
אֲדֹנָי נֶגְדְּךָ כָל־תַּאֲוָתִי:

44

A SERVANT OF GOD

Ah, would that I might be a servant of God,
 my Maker!
Though every friend were far from me, yet He
 would draw me near.

  My Maker, my Shepherd,
  Thou possessest my soul and my body;
  Thou discernest mine aim,
  Thou seest my thoughts,
  My path and my couch;
Ps. 139,2,3. And Thou siftest all my ways.

If Thou help me, who shall make me stumble?
If Thou restrain me, who else can set me free?

  Mine inmost parts do yearn
  To be in communion with Thee,
  While yet my cares
  Set them afar from Thee,
  And my paths incline
  From the path of Thy steps.

Lord, teach me! let me tread along Thy
 truth,
And gently lead me on in judgment and
 condemn me not.

44

עבד אלוה

– – – | – ∪ – | – – – | – ∪ –

עֶבֶד אֱלוֹהַּ עֲשַׂנִי	מִי־יִתְּנֵנִי
כָּל־דּוֹד וְהוּא יַקְרִיבֵנִי:	וִירַחֲקֵנִי
נַפְשִׁי וְגֵוִי קָנִיתָ	יִצְרִי וְרֵעִי
וּמַחְשְׁבוֹתַי רָאִיתָ	בַּנְתָּ לְרֵעִי
וְכָל־דְּרָכַי זֵרִיתָ	אָרְחִי וְרִבְעִי 5
מִי זֶה אֲשֶׁר יַכְשִׁילֵנִי	אִם תַּעְזְרֵנִי
מִי בִלְתְּךָ יַתִּירֵנִי:	אוֹ תַעְצְרֵנִי
לִהְיוֹת קְרֵבִים אֵלֶיךָ	הֵמּוּ קְרֵבַי
יְרַחֲקוּם מֵעָלֶיךָ	אוּלָם עֲצָבַי
מֵעַל נְתִיב מַעְגָּלֶיךָ	יַטּוּ נְתִיבַי 10
בֶּאֱמִתְּךָ הַדְרִיכֵנִי	יָהּ לַמְּדֵנִי
בְּדִין, וְאַל־תַּרְשִׁיעֵנִי:	וּלְאַט נְחֵנִי

If I am even in youth
Too weak to do Thy will,
How then in old age
Can I yet hope and watch?
O God, heal, I beseech Thee!
With Thee, O God, is the healing.

The day old age shall root me up, and my
strength forget me,
Do Thou not leave me, my God; do not
forsake me.

Crushed and weak,
I sit and tremble every moment;
Naked and despoiled,
I go on my vain wanderings;
And I am polluted
Through my manifold sins and trans-
gressions.

Jer. 51,18.

Between Thee and me—iniquity which di-
videth us,
Holding me back from seeing Thy light with
mine eyes.

Incline Thou mine heart
To do the service of Thy kingdom,
And my thought
Make pure for knowledge of Thy God-
ship;
And in my time of pain
O stay Thou not Thine healing.

לַעֲשׂוֹת רְצוֹנְךָ מִתְרַפֵּא   וַאֲנִי בְּעָדְנָה

מַה־זֶּה אֲיַחֵל וַאֲצַפֵּה   אַף כִּי־בְזִקְנָה

כִּי עִמְּךָ אֵל הַמַּרְפֵּא   אֵל נָא רְפָא נָא   15

זִקְנָה וְכֹחִי יַנְשֵׁנִי   יוֹם תִּתְּשֵׁנִי

צוּרִי וְאַל־תַּעַזְבֵנִי: אַל־תִּטְּשֵׁנִי

אֵשֵׁב וְחָרֵד לִרְגָעַי   דַּכָּא וְאֻמְלָל

אֵלֵךְ בְּהַבְלֵי תַעְתּוּעַי   עָרֹם וְשׁוֹלָל

מֵרֹב חֲטָאַי וּפְשָׁעַי   וַאֲנִי מְחֻלָּל   20

עָוֹן אֲשֶׁר יַבְדִּילֵנִי   בֵּינְךָ וּבֵינִי

לִרְאוֹת בְּאוֹרְךָ עֵינִי: וַיַּחְשְׁכֵנִי

לַעֲבֹד עֲבֹדַת מַלְכוּתֶךָ   הַטֵּה לְבָבִי

טַהֵר לְדֵעָה אֱלָהוּתֶךָ   וּמַחֲשָׁבִי

אֵל־נָא תְּאַחֵר רְפֻאוֹתֶךָ   וּבְעֵת כְּאֵבִי   25

Answer, O my God, keep not silence, afflict-
ing me,
Redeem me now, I pray, and say unto Thy
servant: I am here.

אַל־תֶּחֱשֶׁה וּתְעַנֵּנִי   אֵלִי עֲנֵנִי

וָאֹמַר לְעַבְדְּךָ הִנֵּנִי: שֵׁנִית קְנָנִי

45

ASLEEP IN THE BOSOM OF YOUTH

Asleep in the bosom of youth, how long wilt
    thou rest?
Know that boyhood is shaken off like tow.
Are the days of dawn for ever?   Rise, go
    forth—
Prov. 13,24.   See, the angels of old age do chasten thee
    betimes.
Then shake thyself from temporal things, as
    birds
Cant. 5,2.   That shake themselves from the drops of the
    night.
Dart like a swallow to find release from thy
    trespass,
Prov. 27,1.   And from the happenings of the day which
    rage like the ocean.
Pursue after thy King in the intimate com-
    pany
Jer. 31,11.   Of souls that flow unto the goodness of the
    Lord.

45

ישנה בחיק ילדות

רשות

‖ – ‿ – ‿ – ‿ ‖ – ‿ – ‿ – ‿ ‖ – ‿ – ‿ – ‿ ‖

יְשֵׁנָה בְּחֵיק יַלְדוּת לְמָתַי תִּשְׁכְּבִי

דְּעִי כִּי־נְעוּרִים כַּנְּעֹרֶת נִנְעֲרוּ

הֲלָעַד יְמֵי הַשַּׁחֲרוּת קוּמִי צְאִי

רְאִי מַלְאֲכֵי שֵׂיבָה בְּמוּסָר שִׁחֲרוּ

וְהִתְנַעֲרִי מִן־הַזְּמָן כַּצִּפֳּרִים   5

אֲשֶׁר מֵרְסִיסֵי לַיְלָה יִתְנַעֲרוּ

דְּאִי כַדְּרוֹר לִמְצוֹא דְרוֹר מִמַּעֲלָךְ

וּמִתָּלְדוֹת יָמִים כְּיַמִּים יִסְעֲרוּ

הֲיִי אַחֲרֵי מַלְכֵּךְ מְרַדֶּפֶת בְּסוֹד   10

נְשָׁמוֹת אֲשֶׁר אֶל־טוּב אֲדֹנָי נָהֲרוּ:

46

WHO IS LIKE THEE

Job 12,22. Who is like Thee, revealing the deeps,
Ex. 15,11. *Fearful in praises, doing wonders?*

The Creator who discovereth all from nothing,
Is revealed to the heart, but not to the eye;
Therefore ask not how nor where—
Jer. 23,24. *For He filleth heaven and earth.*

Remove lust from the midst of thee;
Job 31,33. Thou wilt find thy God within thy bosom,
Walking gently in thine heart—
I Sam. 2,6. *He that bringeth low and that lifteth up.*

And see the way of the soul's secret;
Search it out and refresh thee.
He will make thee wise, and thou wilt find
  freedom,
 For thou art a captive and the world is a
  prison.

46

מִי כָמוֹךְ

— — — — — —

מִי כָמוֹךָ עֲמֻקוֹת גִּלָּה
נוֹרָא תְהִלֹּת עֹשֵׂה-פֶלֶא:

יוֹצֵר הַמְצִיא כֹל מֵאַיִן
נִגְלָה לְלֵבָב לֹא לָעָיִן
כֵּן אַל-תִּשְׁאַל אֵיךְ וָאַיִן
כִּי שָׁמַיִם וָאָרֶץ מָלֵא:

הָסֵר תַּאֲוָה מִקִּרְבָּךְ
תִּמְצָא צוּרְךָ תּוֹךְ חֻבָּךְ
מִתְהַלֵּךְ לְאַט בִּלְבָבֶךָ
הוּא הַמּוֹרִיד וְהוּא הַמַּעֲלָה:

וּרְאֵה דָרֶךְ סוֹד הַנֶּפֶשׁ
וַחֲקֹר אֹתָהּ וּבָהּ תִּנָּפֵשׁ
הוּא יַשְׂכִּילְךָ וְתִמְצָא חֹפֶשׁ
כִּי אַתְּ אָסִיר וְעוֹלָם כֶּלֶא:

5

10

Make knowledge the envoy between thyself
    and Him;

Aboth 2,4.   Annul thy will and do His will;

And know that wheresoever thou hidest thee,
    there is His eye,

Jer. 32,17.   *And nothing is too hard for Him.*

Prov. 8,24,26.   He was the Living while there was yet no
    dust of the world;

And He is the Maker and He the Bearer;

Isa. 28,4.   And man is counted as a fading flower—

Isa. 34,4.   *Soon to fade, as fadeth a leaf.*

דַּעַת שִׂים צִיר בֵּינְךָ וּבֵינוֹ 15
וּבַטֵּל רְצוֹנְךָ וַעֲשֵׂה רְצוֹנוֹ
וְדַע כִּי בַאֲשֶׁר תַּסְתִּיר עֵינוֹ
וְדָבָר מֶנּוּ לֹא־יִפָּלֵא:

הוּא הַחַי בְּאֵין עַפְרוֹת תֵּבֵל
וְהוּא הָעֹשֶׂה וְהוּא הַסֹּבֵל 20
וְאָדָם נֶחְשָׁב כְּצִיצַת נָבֵל
מַהֵר יִבּוֹל כְּנֵבֶל עָלֶה:

47

HAST THOU FORGOTTEN?

(For rhymed version see page 162)

(For rhymed version see page 162)

Cant. 1,13.

My love, hast Thou forgotten Thy resting
    between my breasts?
And wherefore hast Thou sold me for ever to
    them that enslave me?

Have I not followed Thee of old through a
    land not sown?
Lo, Seir and Mount Paran and Sinai and Sin
    are my witnesses.

And my love was Thine, and Thy favour upon
    me,
And how now hast Thou apportioned my glory
    away from me?

Thrust unto Seir, cast out unto Kedar,
Tested in the furnace of Greece, afflicted under
    the yoke of Media—

Is there, beside Thee, a redeemer or, beside
    me, a captive of hope?—
O give Thy strength to me, for I give Thee
    my love.

47

הַשָׁכַחַת

רשות לנשמת

‖ — — — ‿ | — — — | ‿ — — — | — — — | ‿

חֲנֹתְךָ בְּבֵין שָׁדָי	יְדִידִי הֲשָׁכַחְתָּ
צְמִיתָת לְמַעְבִּידָי	וְלָמָּה מְכַרְתַּנִי
זְרוּעָה רְדַפְתִּיךָ	הֲלֹא אָז בְּאֶרֶץ לֹא
וְסִינַי וְסִין עֵדָי	וְשֵׂעִיר וְהַר־פָּארָן
וְהָיָה רְצוֹנְךָ בִּי	וְהָיוּ לְךָ דוֹדַי
כְּבוֹדִי לְבִלְעָדָי	וְאֵיךְ תַּחֲלַק עַתָּה
הֲדוּפָה עֲדֵי קֵדָר	דְּהֹוּיָה אֱלֵי שֵׂעִיר
מְעֻנָּה בְּעֹל מָדָי	בְּחוֹנָה בְּכוּר יָוָן
וּבִלְתִּי אָסִיר תִּקְוָה	הֲיֵשׁ בִּלְתְּךָ גֹּאֵל
לְךָ אַתָּנֶה דוֹדָי:	תְּנָה־עֻזְּךָ לִי כִּי

5

10

48

THEY THAT KNOW MY SORROW

Job 41,11.   They that know my sorrow add a spark to
    the fire of my heart
Cant. 5,9.   When they ask me: How is thy belovèd more
    precious than another love?

Praises and dark sayings fail to tell of Him;
Dan. 9,23.   He is all desirable; His majesty cannot be
    sought out;
Ezek. 26,16.   Therefore do I clothe myself with terrors at
    His flight.

Ah, pity me, and speak unto the heart so
    moved,
Or comfort me; for how endure love and sepa-
    ration?

Ex. 23,21.   And His name is within me—like fire in my
    reins,
Jer. 20,9.   Bound within my heart, shut up in my bones:
And they rebuke me—they that despise my
    statutes—

And they reproach me when I seek to serve
    Him,
And they revile me when I give glory to His
    Name.

They think to set me far, O God, from Thy
    service:

48

יודעי יגוני
זולת

‖ — — — — | — ◡ — — | — — — ◡ — —

יָסְפוּ בְּאֵשׁ לִבִּי כִידוֹד   יוֹדְעֵי יְגוֹנִי
מַה־נֶּחֱמָד דּוֹדֵךְ מִדּוֹד: כִּי שְׁאָלוּנִי

נִלְאוּ לְהַגִּידוֹ   הֹדֹת וְחִידוֹת
לֹא נֶחֱקַר הוֹדוֹ   כֻּלּוֹ חֲמוּדוֹת
אָלְבַּשׁ עָלַי נוֹדוֹ   עַל־כֵּן חֲרָדוֹת   5

וְדַבְּרוּ עַל־לֵב יְדוֹד   נָא נַחֲמוּנִי
אֵיךְ אוּכְלָה אַהֲבָה וּנְדוֹד: אוֹ רַחֲמוּנִי

כָּאֵשׁ בְּכִלְיוֹתָי   וּשְׁמוֹ בְּקִרְבִּי
עָצַר בְּעַצְמוֹתָי   קָשׁוּר בְּלִבִּי
בּוֹזִים לְחֶקְקוֹתָי   וַיִּגְעֲרוּ בִי   10

יוֹם אֲדָרְשָׁה אֹתוֹ לַעֲבוֹד   וַיְחָרְפוּנִי
כִּי אֶתְּנָה לִשְׁמוֹ כָבוֹד: וַיְנַדְּפוּנִי

אֵל מֵעֲבָדָתְךָ   דָּמוּ לְרַחֲקִי

But my suffering and oppression are better
    than Thine estrangement;
My portion and my pleasure, the sweet fruit
    of Thy law.

Let my right hand forget—if I stand not
    before Thee;
Ps. 137.5-6.   Let my tongue cleave—if I desire aught but
    Thy law.

Lo, in mine ears the sound of Thy praise—
The Red Sea and Sinai are witnesses to Thy
    greatness:
How shall my thoughts dwell on any but Thee?

My heart and mine eyes will not suffer my
    feet to slip,
For this, the Lord, is One; there is none be-
    side Him.

לַחְצִי וְדָחְקִי טוֹב מִפְּרִידָתֶךְ
חֶלְקִי וְחִשְׁקִי נֹעַם פְּרִי דָתֶךְ
תִּשְׁכַּח יְמִינִי אִם־לֹא לְפָנֶיךָ אֶעֱמֹד
תִּדְבַּק לְשׁוֹנִי אִם בִּלְעֲדֵי דָתֶךְ אֶחֱמֹד:

הִנֵּה בְּאָזְנִי שְׁמַע תְּהִלָּתֶךְ
יַם־סוּף וְסִינַי עֵדִי גְדֻלָּתֶךְ
אֵיךְ רַעֲיוֹנִי יָהְגוּ בְזוּלָתֶךְ
לִבִּי וְעֵינִי לֹא־יִתְּנוּ רַגְלַי לִמְעוֹד
כִּי־זֶה אֲדֹנָי אֶחָד וְזוּלָתוֹ אֵין עוֹד:

49

REDEMPTION

<table>
<tr><td>Ex. 19,4.</td><td>The dove Thou hast borne on eagles' wings,
That hath nested in Thy bosom in the inner-
    most chambers—
Why hast Thou left her flying about the forest</td></tr>
<tr><td>Isa. 19,8.</td><td>While on every side are spreaders of nets?
Strangers entice her with other gods,</td></tr>
<tr><td>Jer. 13,17.</td><td>But she in secret weepeth for the lord of her
    youth.
And Dishan and Dishon[1] speak smoothly
    to her,</td></tr>
<tr><td>Hos. 2,9.</td><td>But she lifteth her eyes to her first husband:—</td></tr>
<tr><td>Ps. 16,10.</td><td>Why hast Thou abandoned my soul to the
    grave—</td></tr>
<tr><td>Ruth 4,4.</td><td>While I know there is none beside Thee
    to redeem?</td></tr>
<tr><td>Cant. 5,2;6,9.
Isa.47,2.</td><td>Shall she that was undefiled go ever with
        uncovered locks,
A contempt and appalment to Mizzah and
    Shammah?[2]
Lo, the bondwoman's son[3] hath spread terror
    for me,</td></tr>
<tr><td>Ps. 78,9.</td><td>For with hand upraised he shot with the bow.</td></tr>
</table>

[1] Horites, inhabitants of Edom. (Gen.36,21).

[2] Edomites, grandsons of Esau. (Gen.36,13).

[3] Ishmael. (Gen.21,10). Note the play with the names of the nations mentioned.

49

אין זולתך לגאול
גאולה

עַל-כַּנְפֵי נְשָׁרִים   יוֹנָה נְשָׂאתָה
בְּחַדְרֵי חֲדָרִים   וְקִנְנָה בְחֵיקֶךָ
נוֹדְדָה בַיְעָרִים   לָמָה נְטַשְׁתָּהּ
פֹּרְשֵׂי מַכְמֹרִים   וּמִכֹּל עֲבָרִים
בֵּאלֹהִים אֲחֵרִים   יְסִיתוּהָ זָרִים   5
תִּבְכֶּה לְבַעַל נְעוּרִים   וְהִיא בְמִסְתָּרִים

יַחֲלִיק לָהּ לָשׁוֹן   וּבְדִישָׁן וְדִישׁוֹן
לְאִישָׁהּ הָרִאשׁוֹן   וְתִשָּׂא אִישׁוֹן
נַפְשִׁי לִשְׁאוֹל   לָמָה תַעֲזֹב
זוּלָתְךָ לִגְאוֹל: וְאֵדְעָה כִּי אֵין   10

תְּהִי גָּלוּת צָמָה   הֲלָנֶצַח תַּמָּה
לְמָזֶה וְשַׁמָּה   בִּזָּה וְשַׁמָּה
הֶעֱטַנִי אֵימָה   וּבָךְ הָאָמָה
קֶשֶׁת רָמָה   כִּי בְיָד רָמָה

And my tent became a high place for Oholi-
    bamah,[1]
And Oholibah[2]—how shall she still hope, and
    how long?
    Since there is no miracle and no sign, no
      vision, no sight—

Dan. 12.6.   And should I ask to behold when shall be
    the end of these wonders,
II Kings 2,10.   The prophecies answer: Thou hast asked
    a hard thing.

    The daughters lapped in luxury are exiled
      from their homes,
Isa. 32,18.   From green couches and quiet resting places,
Isa. 27,11.   And scattered amid peoples of no understand-
    ing,
Isa. 28,11.   Of strange lips and other tongues;
    Yet have they kept the faith, nurtured among
      these,
Ex. 10,3.   And to pictured idols have refused to humble
    themselves.
Ps. 10,1.   Then why standeth He afar off that dwelleth
    in the skies,
    While my ruler oppresseth and my belovèd
    is afar?[3]
Neh. 13,6.   And as for the end of days—verily one
I Sam. 20,6,28   asketh!

[1] Wife of Esau. (Gen.36, 2,5,18).
[2] Jerusalem. (Ezek.23,4). Note the deft play on
words in lines 15 and 16.
[3] Note the play by transposition of letters.

15

וְאָהֳלִי בָמָה   לְאָהֳלִיבָמָה

וְאָהֳלִיבָה מַה־   תִּיַחֵל עוֹד וְכַמָּה

וְאֵיךְ מוֹפֵת וְאֵין רְאוֹת   וְאֵין חָזוֹן וּמַרְאוֹת

וְאִם־אֶשְׁאַל לִרְאוֹת   מָתַי קֵץ הַפְּלָאוֹת

יַעֲנוּ נְבוּאוֹת   הִקְשִׁיתָ לִשְׁאוֹל:

20

וּבָנוֹת עֲדִינוֹת   הָגְלוּ מִמְּדִינוֹת

מִמְּטוֹת רַעֲנַנּוֹת   וּמְנוּחֹת שַׁאֲנַנּוֹת

וְנִפְזְרוּ בֵינוֹת   עַם לֹא־בִינוֹת

בְּלַעֲגֵי שָׂפָה   וּבִלְשֹׁנוֹת שֹׁנוֹת

אַךְ שָׁמְרוּ אֱמוּנוֹת   בָּם הָיוּ אֱמוּנוֹת

וְלָאֱלִילֵי תְמוּנוֹת   מֵאֲנוּ לַעֲנוֹת   25

וְלָמָה בַמֶּרְחָק   עָמַד דָּר שָׁחַק

וְרוֹדִי דָחַק   וְדוֹדִי רָחַק

וּלְקֵץ יָמִים   נִשְׁאַל נִשְׁאוֹל:

The banner of brotherhood is removed from
    me

Isa. 52,2. And the foot of pride is yoke and band upon
    me;[1]

Jer. 30,14. And I am chastened with cruel castigation,

Exiled and prisoned, vexed and thrust away;

Nah. 3,17. Without marshal or chief, without king or
Hos. 3,4.   prince,

While the foe turneth towards me, and my
    Rock turneth away.

Deut. 2,5.   He hath ruined in His wrath the Place of
    His foot-steps,

And burnt in His indignation His doorposts
    and His threshold,

Deut. 32,22. And a fire is kindled in His anger that
    burneth unto Sheol.

Ps. 77,8. Will the Lord reject for ever?

Dan. 8,19. Is there no end to the times appointed of my
    dreams?

Num. 10,35. Rise up, O Lord, and let mine adversaries be
    scattered,

And return to mine habitations, to the inner-
    most shrine;

Reveal to mine eyes Thy glory as from Sinai,

Ps.79,12; 94,2. And requite upon them that reproached me[2]
    a recompense for my sorrow.

----

[1] The idea is of the foot being placed on the neck of the
fallen foe.

[2] Ps.79,4;44,14. Jehudah Halevi most probably had
the sense of these verses in mind when using the word
"neighbours".

דָּגְל אַחֲוָה　　　　　מֵעָלַי הוּסָר

וְרֶגֶל גַּאֲוָה　　　　　עָלַי עָל וּמוֹסָר　　30

וַאֲנִי מְיֻסָּר　　　　　בְּאַכְזְרִיּוּת מוּסָר

גֹּלָה וְנֶאֱסָר　　　　　חֲצֵף וָסָר

בְּאֵין מִנְזָר וְטִפְסָר　　　　וְאֵין מֶלֶךְ וְאֵין שָׂר

וְצָר אֵלַי סָר　　　　　וְצוּר מִנִּי סָר

וְהֶחֱרִיב בְּקִצְפּוֹ　　　　מָקוֹם מִדְרַךְ כַּפּוֹ　　35

וְהִצִּית בְּזַעְפּוֹ　　　　מְזוּזָתוֹ וְסִפּוֹ

וְאֵשׁ קָדְחָה בְאַפּוֹ　　　　וַתִּיקַד עַד־שְׁאוֹל:

הַלְעוֹלָמִים　　　　　יִזְנַח אֲדֹנָי

וְהַאֵין קֵצָה　　　　　לְמוֹעֲדֵי חֶזְיוֹנִי

קוּמָה אֲדֹנִי　　　　　וְיָפֻצוּ שֹׂטְנָי　　40

וְשׁוּב אֱלִי־מְעוֹנִי　　　　אֱלֵי־הֵיכַל לְפָנַי

וְנִגְלָה לְעֵינַי　　　　כְּבוֹדְךָ כְּמִסִּינַי

וְהָשֵׁב לְשֹׁכְנַי　　　　גְּמוּל עַל־יְגוֹנַי

With dew of salvation descend upon him
 that feareth and trembleth
And bring low from his throne the bold son
 of the bondwoman,
Gen.42,38;44,31. Speedily—lest I go down in sorrow to the
 grave.

עַל־יְיָרֵא וְחָרַד   וּבְטַל־יֶשַׁע רַד
בָּן־הָאָמָה מְרַד   וּמִכִּסְאוֹ הוֹרַד   45
בְּיָגוֹן אֶל־שְׁאוֹל: מְהֵרָה פָּן־אֶרַד

50

A LAMENT

Lam. 2,15.	How is she that was wholly beautiful dis- guised to the eyes of all flesh—
Jer. 15,9.	Her sun gone down while yet it is day, the desire of her eyes removed!
	Her Lord hath rebuked her and set her in bonds,
Hos. 3,4.	*Without king and without prince.*

Hotly have foes pursued her, have wakened
    against her with hatred,

Jer. 38,22.   Have sunk her feet in the mire: she hath
Isa. 50,11.   lain down in sorrow.
Ezek. 26,17. And the lauded city is left waste like the wilder-
      ness,
Hos. 3,4.   *Without sacrifice and without pillar.*

Isa. 25,5.   Branches of the terrible ones are gathered to
Ps. 40,15.   sweep her away;
Ezek. 8,17. Her seasons change, her sorrows are changeless.
     Lions have torn her, her griefs are laid bare,
Hos. 3,4.   *Without Ephod and Teraphim.*

Thou, only One, give rest to her, that a
    remnant may be left in her,

II Kings 19,3. For children are come to the birth, but there
Isa. 37,3.   is no strength to bring forth.
    Be a shield about them in thy mercy, Almighty
    Ruler!

50

איכה כלילת יופי

קרובה

אֵיכָה כְּלִילַת יֹפִי מִתְנַכְּרָה לְעֵין כָּל־בָּשָׂר

בָּא שִׁמְשָׁהּ בְּעֹד יוֹמָם וּמַחְמַד עֵינֶיהָ הוּסָר

גָּעַר בָּהּ בַּעֲלָהּ וַיִּתְּנָהּ בְּמַאְסָר

אֵין מֶלֶךְ וְאֵין שָׂר:

דָּלְקוּהָ אוֹיְבִים וַיְעוֹרְרוּ עָלֶיהָ אֵיבָה   5

הָטְבְּעוּ בַבּוֹץ רַגְלֶיהָ וַתִּשְׁכַּב לְמַעֲצֵבָה

וְהָעִיר הַהֲלָלָה נוֹתָרָה כְּמִדְבָּר חֲרֵבָה

אֵין זֶבַח וְאֵין מַצֵּבָה:

זְמִירֵי עָרִיצִים לְסִפּוֹתָהּ נֶאֱסָפִים

חָלְפוּ זְמַנֶּיהָ וְיגוֹנֶיהָ לֹא נֶחֱלָפִים   10

טָרְפוּהָ לְבָאִים וּמַכְאֹבֶיהָ נֶחֱשָׁפִים

אֵין אֵפוֹד וּתְרָפִים:

כרוז

יָחִיד הֵנָּחֵם לְהוֹתִיר לָהּ פָּלִיט

כִּי־בָאוּ בָנִים עַד־מַשְׁבֵּר וְכֹחַ אַיִן לְהַפְלִיט

לְגוֹנֵן עֲלֵיהֶם בְּרַחֲמֶיךָ שַׁדַּי הַשַּׁלִּיט   15

Isa. 31,5.   Shielding, He will deliver: passing over, He will rescue.

Isa. 42,24.   Who hath given Jacob for a spoil at the ends of the world,
Forsaken like a ship in the heart of the sea—
    lost without a pilot?
Est. 6,12.   We lament in our exile with covered head and mourning,
Ps. 137,1.   *By the rivers of Babylon.*
Lam. 2,11.   By the rivers of Babylon our eyes are consumed with tears.
Ezek. 23,4.   We have taken account of thee, Oholibah; we have remembered Oholah.
Ps. 137,2.   We have silenced the loud sounding cymbals, we have hung up our harps:
Ps. 137,1.   *There we sat down, yea, we wept.*

We have called to the wailing until even owls have no semblance to us;
So many are our sighs for the burning of the Shrine of the Most High.
Wide grew our breach, we were all but a ruin—
Ps. 137,1.   *When we remembered Zion.*

Let our right hand forget, if we forget thee,
Ps. 137,5   O Jerusalem!
The days of thy majesty and the goal of thy release we have hoped from heaven.
We cast ourselves down before God, and our eyelids run down with water—
Hos. 6,2.   After two days He will revive us.

גָּנוֹן וְהַצִּיל פָּסוֹחַ וְהַמְלִיט:

מחיה

מִי־נָתַן לִמְשִׁסָּה יַעֲקֹב בְּקַצְוֵי תֵבֵל
נֶעֱזָב כָּאֳנִי בְלֶב־יָם מִבְּלִי חֹבֵל
סָפַדְנוּ בְגָלוּתֵנוּ חֲפוּי רֹאשׁ וְאָבֵל
עַל־נַהֲרוֹת בָּבֶל:

עַל נַהֲרוֹת בָּבֶל עֵינֵינוּ בַּדְּמָעוֹת כָּלִינוּ
פְּקַדְנוּךְ אֹהֲלִיבָה וְאָהֳלָה עַל־לֵב הֶעֱלִינוּ
צַלְצַלֵי־שֵׁמַע הֶחֱרַשְׁנוּ וְכִנּוֹרוֹתֵינוּ תָּלִינוּ
שָׁם יָשַׁבְנוּ גַּם־בָּכִינוּ:

קָרָאנוּ לִנְהִי עַד אֵין לָנוּ בִּבְנוֹת יַעֲנָה דִמְיוֹן
רַבּוּ אַנְחוֹתֵינוּ עַל־שְׂרֵפַת מִקְדַּשׁ עֶלְיוֹן
שֻׁבַּרְנוּ גַדֵל וְכִמְעַט הָיִינוּ לְכִלְיוֹן
בְּזָכְרֵנוּ אֶת־צִיּוֹן:

כרוג

תִּשְׁכַּח יְמִינֵנוּ אִם־נִשְׁכָּחֵךְ יְרוּשָׁלַיִם
יְמֵי הוֹרֵךְ וְקֵץ דְּ־רוֹרֵךְ הוֹחַלְנוּ מִשָּׁמַיִם
הִתְנַפַּלְנוּ לְפָנֶי־אֵל וְעַפְעַפֵּינוּ יִזְּלוּ־מָיִם
יְחַיֵּנוּ מִיָּמָיִם:

20

25

30

51

MY SHAME IS MY GLORY

With all my heart, in truth, and with all my
    might,
Have I loved Thee.   In open and in secret
Thy name is with me: how shall I go alone?
(Yea, He is my belovèd: how shall I sit
    solitary?
And He is my lamp: how shall my light be
    quenched?
And how shall I halt, since He is a staff in
    my hand?)
Men have held me in contempt, knowing not
That my shame for Thy name's glory is my
    glory.—
O Fount of my life!   I will bless Thee while
    I live,
And sing Thee my song while being is mine.

51

קלוני על כבוד שמך כבודי

‖ – – – | ‿ – | – – – | ‿

בְּכָל־לִבִּי אֱמֶת וּבְכָל־מְאֹדִי

אֲהַבְתִּיךָ וּבְגִלּוּיִי וְסוֹדִי

שְׁמָךְ נֶגְדִּי וְאֵיךְ אֵלֵךְ לְבַדִּי

וְהוּא דוֹדִי וְאֵיךְ אֵשֵׁב יְחִידִי

וְהוּא נֵרִי וְאֵיךְ יִדְעַךְ מְאוֹרִי   5

וְאֵיךְ אֶצְעַן וְהוּא מִשְׁעָן בְּיָדִי

הֲקָלוּנִי מְתִים לֹא יָדְעוּ כִּי

קָלוֹנִי עַל־כְּבוֹד שְׁמָךְ כְּבוֹדִי

מְקוֹר חַיַּי אֲבָרֶכְךָ בְחַיָּי

וְזִמְרָתִי אֲזַמָּרְךָ בְעוֹדִי: 10

52

THOU WHO KNOWEST OUR SORROWS

Ps. 147,3.
Thou who knowest our sorrows, and bindest
up our wounds,
Turn again our tens of thousands to the land
of our abodes.
There shall we offer our oblations, our vows,
our freewill offerings,
There shall we make before Thee the offerings
due to Thee.

The faithful recall to-day the wonders of
olden time;
The children groan, for other lords beside Thee
are their masters.
Where is God's covenant to the fathers, where
His former mercies,
When He spake from the heaven of His
dwelling, unto us, face to face,
When He gave into the hand of the faithful
envoy the two tablets of stone?
And where are all His marvels which our
fathers have told us?

How long have we drunken our fill of bitter-
ness, and hoped for Thy salvation?
How many seasons were we sick with longing,
but entreated none but Thee,
And watched for the light of morning, but
were covered with thick darkness?

52

יֵדַע מַכְאוֹבֵינוּ

פזמון למצות עשה

‒ ‒ ‒ ‒ ‒ ‒ | ‒ ‒ ‒ ‒ ‒ ‒

וּמְחַבֵּשׁ לְעַצְּבוֹתֵינוּ · יֵדַע מַכְאוֹבֵינוּ
אֶל־אֶרֶץ מוֹשָׁבֹתֵינוּ · שׁוּבָה אֶת־דְּרָבְבוֹתֵינוּ
נְדָרֵינוּ וְנִדְבֹתֵינוּ · וְשָׁם נַעֲלֶה עֹלֹתֵינוּ
אֶת־קָרְבְּנוֹת חוֹבֹתֵינוּ: · וְשָׁם נַעֲשֶׂה לְפָנֶיךָ

הַפְּלָאִים הַקַּדְמוֹנִים · הִזְכִּירוּ הַיּוֹם אֱמוּנִים 5
בְּעָלוֹם זוּלָתְךָ אֲדֹנִים · וַיֵּאָנְחוּ הַבָּנִים
וַחֲסָדָיו הָרִאשֹׁנִים · אַיֵּה בְּרִית־אֵל לָאֵתָנִים
עִמָּנוּ פָנִים בְּפָנִים · בְּדַבְּרוֹ מִשְּׁמֵי מְעוֹנִים
אֶת־שְׁנֵי לוּחֹת הָאֲבָנִים · וּבְכָתְבוֹ בְּיַד צִיר אֱמוּנִים
סִפְּרוּ־לָנוּ אֲבוֹתֵינוּ: · וְאַיֵּה כָל־נִפְלְאוֹתָיו אֲשֶׁר 10

וְלִישׁוּעָתְךָ קִוִּינוּ · וְכַמָּה מְרֹרוֹת רֻוֵּינוּ
וְזוּלָתְךָ לֹא חָלִינוּ · וְכַמָּה זְמַנִּים חָלִינוּ
וּבְמַחֲשַׁכִּים נִטְמֵינוּ · וּלְאוֹר בֹּקֶר חִכִּינוּ

As though we had not been a People, nay,
    had not been more wonderful than any
    People;
As though we had not seen the day of Sinai,
    nor had drunken the waters of the rock,
And Thy manna had not been in our mouth,
    and Thy cloud about us!

They ask the way to Zion—they pray toward
    her—
The children exiled from her border, but which
    have not stript themselves of their adorn-
    ment.
The beautiful adornment for which they were
    praised, for this they are slain and defiled—
The treasures they inherited at Horeb, whereby
    they are justified and proud;
Slaves bear rule over them, but they will never
    cease to call Thee
Until Thou turn our captivity and comfort our
    waste places.

We stand upon our watch to keep Thy right-
    eous judgments—
And even if our splendour be ruined, and we
    be thrust forth from Thy bosom,
And an handmaid be our mistress, and those
    far off from Thee rule over us,
Yet do we hold fast to our crown, the diadem
    of Thy statutes,
Until Thou gather our company into the house
    of Thy choice and Thy desire,
Our holy place, our glory, where our fathers
    praised Thee.

כְּאִלּוּ עָם לֹא הָיִינוּ   וּמִכָּל־עָם לֹא נִפְלֵינוּ

15   וְיוֹם סִינַי לֹא רָאִינוּ   וּמִי הַצּוּר לֹא שָׁתִינוּ

וְלֹא הָיָה מִנְּךָ בְּפִינוּ   וַעֲנָנְךָ סְבִיבֹתֵינוּ׃

דָּרֵךְ צִיּוֹן יִשְׁאָלוּ   וְאֵלֶיהָ יִתְפַּלָּלוּ

בָּנִים מִגְּבוּלָם גָּלוּ   וְעָדִים לֹא הִתְנַצָּלוּ

עֲדָיֵהֶן אֲשֶׁר בּוֹ הֻלָּלוּ   עָלָיו הֹרְגוּ וְחֹלָּלוּ

20   חֲמָדוֹת בְּחֹרֶב נָחָלוּ   בָּם יִצְדְּקוּ וְיִתְהַלָּלוּ

עֲבָדִים בָּהֶם מָשָׁלוּ   וּמִקְרָא לְךָ לֹא יָחְדָּלוּ

עַד אֲשֶׁר תָּשִׁיב שְׁבוּתֵינוּ   וּתְנַחֵם חָרְבֹתֵינוּ׃

הֶעֱמַדְנוּ מִשְׁמַרְתֵּנוּ   לִשְׁמֹר מִשְׁפְּטֵי צִדְקָךְ

וְאִם שָׁדְדָה אַדַּרְתֵּנוּ   וְנִגְרַשְׁנוּ מֵחֵיקָךְ

25   וְהָיְתָה שִׁפְחָה גְּבִרְתֵּנוּ   וּמָשְׁלוּ בָנוּ רְחֵקָיךְ

הֶחֱזַקְנוּ בַּעֲטַרְתֵּנוּ   נֵזֶר צְפִירַת חֻקָּיךְ

עַד תֶּאֱסֹף מַחְבַּרְתֵּנוּ   לְבֵית בְּחִירָתָךְ וְחִשְׁקָךְ

קִדַּשְׁנוּ וְתִפְאַרְתֵּנוּ   אֲשֶׁר הִלְּלוּךְ אֲבֹתֵינוּ׃

53

TO THE SOUL

The precious one abiding in her body,
As light abideth in deep darkness—
Longeth she not to separate from the body,
And return to the majesty of her trappings?
For she shall eat, on the day of her separation,
The fruit of her law[1]—and this is the fruit
    thereof:
Honey of Eden, a honeycomb of sweetness,

Ps. 103,5.   To satisfy her mouth with good things.

The ways of her Maker she shall see,
And shall forget the days of her affliction;
She shall praise His Name with all
The souls that be praising God.

[1] The reward of her observance of the Torah. Note
play on the words פרידתה and פרי דתה.

53

יקרה שכנה גויה

‖ – – – | – – ‿ –

כְּאוֹר יִשְׁכֹּן בְּמַאְפֵּלְיָה	יְקָרָה שָׁכְנָה גְוֵיָה
וְלָשׁוּב אֶל־גְּאוֹן עֶדְיָה	הֲלֹא תַחְמֹד פְּרִידַת גֵּו
פְּרִי דָתָהּ–וְזֶה־פִּרְיָהּ	וְתֹאכַל יוֹם פְּרִידָתָהּ
לְהַשְׂבִּיעַ בְּטוֹב עֶדְיָהּ	דְּבַשׁ־עֵדֶן וְצוּף־נֹעַם
וְתִשְׁכַּח אֶת־יְמֵי עָנְיָהּ	הֲלִיכוֹת יְצָרָהּ תִּרְאֶה
נְשָׁמָה שֶׁתְּהַלַּל יָהּ:	תְּהַלַּל אֶת־שְׁמוֹ עִם־כָּל

5

54

LET THY FAVOUR PASS TO ME

Let Thy favour pass to me,
Even as Thy wrath hath passed;
Shall mine iniquity for ever
Stand between me and Thee?
How long shall I search
For Thee beside me, and find Thee not?
O Dweller amid the wings of the Cherubim
That are outspread over Thine Ark,
Thou hast enslaved me unto strangers
While I am the man of Thy right hand.
My Redeemer! to redeem my multitudes
Rise and look forth from Thine abiding place.

Ps. 80,16.

54

יעבור עלי רצונך

גאולה

— — ◡ — | — ◡ — —

כַּאֲשֶׁר עָבַר חֲרוֹנֶךְ	יַעֲבֹר עָלַי רְצוֹנֶךְ
יַעֲמֹד בֵּינִי וּבֵינֶךְ	הַלְעוֹלָמִים עֲוֹנִי
אִתְּךָ עִמִּי–וְאֵינֶךְ	וַעֲדֵי מָתַי אֲבַקֵּשׁ
הַפֹּרְשִׂים עַל-אֲרוֹנֶךְ	דָּר בְּכַנְפֵי הַכְּרֻבִים
וַאֲנִי כַּנַּת יְמִינֶךְ	הֶעֱבַדְתַּנִי לְזָרִים–
רָם וְהַשְׁקֵף מִמְּעוֹנֶךְ:	גֹּאֲלִי לִגְאוֹל הֲמוֹנִי

5

55

ACQUAINTED WITH TRUTH

Thou, acquainted with truth, cast out the
    false,
And dwell in the world as though dwelling in
    durance.
Thine honour and thy majesty—to serve God
    while thou livest,
And to leave worldly honour to others.
It is well if thou wake the dawn to serve Him
And sleep not so long that the dawn wake thee.
Know thy tomorrow while thy today lasteth,
And fear not to leave the earth to strangers.
Is it not better far for thee to minister
    before God
Than to be ministering unto mortals—
Before God, whose memory and whose name
Every soul praiseth with joy and songs?

55

יְדוּעַת אמונות
לשמיני עצרת

‿ – – ‿ | – – ‿ | – – ‿ | – – ‿

יְדוּעַת אֱמוּנוֹת דְּחִי הַשְּׁקָרִים
וְשִׁכְנִי בְתֵבֵל כְּשׁכְנֵי קְבָרִים

הֲדָרֵךְ וְהוֹדֵךְ עֲבֹד אֵל בְּעוֹדֵךְ
וְלַעֲזֹב הֲדַר הַזְּמָן לַאֲחֵרִים

וְטוֹב כִּי תָעִירִין שְׁחָרִים לְעָבְדוֹ
וְאַל תִּישְׁנִי עַד יְעִירוּךְ שְׁחָרִים

דְּעִי מָחֳרָתֵךְ בְּיוֹמֵךְ וְאַל־תִּפְּ־
חֲדִי מֵעֲזֹב הָאֲדָמָה לְזָרִים

הֲלֹא טוֹב הֱיוֹתֵךְ מְשָׁרַת פְּנִי־אֵל
מְאֹד מֵהְיוֹתֵךְ מְשָׁרַת פְּגָרִים

פְּנִי־אֵל אֲשֶׁר כָּל־נְשָׁמָה תְהַלֵּל
לְזִכְרוֹ וְלִשְׁמוֹ בְּשִׂמְחָה וְשִׁירִים:

56

WAKE ME TO BLESS THY NAME

Thou didst know me before Thou hadst formed
    me,
And so long as Thy spirit is within me, Thou
    keepest me.
Have I any standing ground if Thou drive
    me out?
Is there any going forth for me if Thou re-
    strain me?
And what can I say, since my thought is in
    Thine hand?
And what can I do until Thou help me?
I have sought Thee: in a time of favour
    answer me,
And as with a shield, gird me round with Thy
    grace.
Raise me up to seek early Thy shrine;
Wake me to bless Thy name.

56

את שמך לברך עוררני
בקשה לשחרית

‖ ‒ ‒ | ◡ ‒ ‒ | ‒ ‒ | ◡ ‒ ◡

יְדַעְתַּנִי בְּטֶרֶם תִּצְרֵנִי
וְכָל־עוֹד רוּחֲךָ בִּי תִּצְרֵנִי

הֲיֵשׁ־לִי מַעֲמָד אִם־תָּהְדְּפֵנִי
וְאִם לִי מַהֲלָךְ אִם־תַּעְצְרֵנִי

וּמָה אֹמַר וּמַחְשָׁבִי בְּיָדְךָ
וּמָה אוּכַל עֲשׂה עַד־תַּעְזְרֵנִי   5

דְּרַשְׁתִּיךָ בְּעֵת רָצוֹן עֲנֵנִי
וְכָצְנֶה רְצוֹנְךָ תַּעְטְרֵנִי

הֲקִימֵנִי לְשַׁחַר אֶת־דְּבִירָךְ
וְאֶת־שִׁמְךָ לְבָרֵךְ עוֹרֲרֵנִי: 10

57

RADIANCE

Day and night (praise the Lord!)
He maketh His face to shine over against my
    face.
He kindled lamps of light, and the darkness
    moved
On the day He rent open my windows in the
    sky.
And He deigned to set of His radiance upon me,
His spirit speaking within me by the hand of
    my faithful.[1]
By the way the light streamed He led me,
The day He came from Seir and shone forth
    from Sinai;
And when I tasted the honey of His law, I
    spake:
Come ye now and see, for mine eyes are
    full of light!

Ps. 89,38.
Num. 12,7.
I Sam. 3,20.
Deut. 33,2.

---

[1] Referring to בכל ביתי נאמן הוא (Numbers 12,7) and
possibly to Ps. 19,8, with regard to the precepts.

57

כי ארו עיני

יוצר

— — — — — — —

יוֹמָם וָלַיְלָה הַלֵּל לַאדֹנָי

הָאִיר אוֹר פָּנָיו אֶל־עֵבֶר פָּנַי

הֶעֱלָה נֵרוֹת אוֹר וַיָּמֶשׁ חֹשֶׁךְ

יוֹם בָּרָקִיעַ קָרַע חַלּוֹנַי

וַיּוֹאֶל לָתֵת מֵהוֹדוֹ עָלַי   5

רוּחוֹ דְבָרִ־בִּי עַל־יַד נֶאֱמָנַי

דֶּרֶךְ יַחֲלָק אוֹר הִדְרִיכַנִי

עֵת זָרַח מִשֵּׂעִיר בָּא מִסִּינַי

הָעֵת טָעַמְתִּי צוּף דָּתוֹ שַׁחְתִּי

בְּאַרְנָא וּרְאוּ כִּי־אָרוּ עֵינָי: 10

58

THE PHYSICIAN'S PRAYER

My God, heal me and I shall be healed,
Let not Thine anger be kindled against me
    so that I be consumed.
My medicines are of Thee, whether good
Or evil, whether strong or weak.
It is Thou who shalt choose, not I;[1]
Of Thy knowledge is the evil and the fair.
Not upon my power of healing I rely;
Only for Thine healing do I watch.

[1] S. D. Luzzatto says here, '"not *I*" instead of "not the physician" because Jehudah Halevi himself was the physician.'

58

אלי רפאני

בשתותו סם רפואה

‖ – – | ⏑ – | – – ‖ – – | ⏑ – |

אֵלִי רְפָאֵנִי וְאֵרָפֵא

אַל־יֶחֱרֶה אַפְּךָ וְאֶסָּפֶה

סַמִּי וּמָרְקָחִי לְךָ בֵּין טוֹב

בֵּין רָע וּבֵין חָזָק וּבֵין רָפֶה

אַתָּה אֲשֶׁר תִּבְחַר וְלֹא אָנִי   5

עַל־דַּעְתְּךָ הָרָע וְהַיָּפֶה

לֹא עַל־רְפוּאָתִי אֲנִי נִסְמָךְ

רַק אָל־רְפוּאָתְךָ אֲנִי צֹפֶה:

59

MINE ONLY ONE

Mine only one, seek God early on His thresh-
  hold,
And, like incense, give thy song to His nostrils.
Lo, if thou pursue the vanities of thy time,
And say that all its witcheries are truth,
And if thou drift thereafter all thy nights and
  thy days,
And the slumber of its dawns be sweet to thee—
Know that there is naught in thine hands
But only a tree whose boughs will wither
  tomorrow.
Abide before thy God and thy King,
Ruth 2,12. Under whose wings thou art come to take
  refuge,
Whose name is magnified and sanctified in the
  mouth of all
That breathe with the breath of the living God.

59

יחידה
רשות לנשמת

‖ ‿ — — | — — — | — ‿ — |

יְחִידָה שַׁחֲרִי הָאֵל וְסַפִּיו
וְכִקְטֹרֶת תְּנִי שִׁירֵךְ בְּאַפִּיו

הֲלֹא אִם־תִּרְדְּפִי הַבְלֵי זְמַנֵּךְ
וְתֹאמְרִי כִּי־אֱמֶת הֵם כָּל־כְּשָׁפָיו

וְתֵזְלִי אַחֲרָיו לֵילֵךְ וְיוֹמֵךְ
וְתָעֳרַב לָךְ תְּנוּמָה מִנְשָׁפָיו   5

דְּעִי כִּי־אֵין בְּיָדַיִךְ מְאוּמָה
אֲבָל עֵץ יָבְשׁוּ מָחָר עֲנָפָיו

הֲיִי לִפְנֵי אֱלֹהַיִךְ וּמַלְכֵּךְ
אֲשֶׁר־בָּאת לַחֲסוֹת תַּחַת־כְּנָפָיו   10

שְׁמוֹ יֻגְדַּל וְיִתְקַדַּשׁ בְּפִי כֹל
אֲשֶׁר נִשְׁמַת אֱלוֹהַּ חַי בְּאַפָּיו:

60

VISION OF GOD

(For rhymed version see page 164)

To meet the fountain of the life of truth I run,
For I weary of a life of vanity and emptiness.
To see the face of my King is mine only aim;
Isa. 8,12.   I will fear none but Him, nor set up any other
      to be feared.
Would that it were mine to see Him in a dream!
I would sleep an everlasting sleep and never
      wake.
Would I might behold His face within my heart!
Mine eyes would never ask to look beyond.

60

לו אחזה פניו

‏– – – ‎‏|‏ – ⌣ – ‎‏|‏ – ⌣ – ‎‏|‏ – ⌣ – – ‏‏

לִקְרַאת מְקוֹר חַיֵּי אֱמֶת אָרוּצָה

עַל־כֵּן בְּחַיֵּי שָׁוְא וָרִיק אָקוּצָה

לִרְאוֹת פְּנֵי מַלְכִּי מְגַמָּתִי לְבָד

לֹא אֶעֱרָץ בִּלְתּוֹ וְלֹא אַעֲרִיצָה

מִי־יִתְּנֵנִי לַחֲזוֹתוֹ בַּחֲלוֹם

אִישַׁן שְׁנַת־עוֹלָם וְלֹא אָקִיצָה

לוּ אֶחֱזֶה פָנָיו בְּלִבִּי בָיְתָה

לֹא שָׁאֲלוּ עֵינַי לְהַבִּיט חוּצָה:

61

YE CURTAINS OF SOLOMON

Ye curtains of Solomon, how, amid the tents
    of Kedar,
Are ye changed?   Ye have no form, no beauty!

"The multitudes which dwelt aforetime in our
    midst,
Have left us a desolation, a broken ruin,
    unprotected—
The holy vessels have gone into exile and be-
    come profane,
And how can ye ask for beauty of a lily
    among thorns?"

Rejected of their neighbours, but sought of
    their Lord,
Isa. 40,26.   He will call them each by name; not one
    shall be missing.
Their beauty, as in the beginning, He shall
    restore in the end,
And shall illume as the sevenfold light their
    lamp which is darkened.

61

יְרִיעוֹת שלמה

מאורה

‒ ‒ ‒ ∪ | ‒ ∪ | ‒ ‒ | ‒ ‒ ∪ | ‒ ∪ | ‒ ‒ | ‖

בְּתוֹךְ אָהֳלֵי קֵדָר	יְרִיעוֹת שְׁלֹמֹה, אֵיךְ
עֲלֵיכֶם וְלֹא הָדָר	שְׁנִיתֶם, וְלֹא תֹאַר
לְפָנִים בְּתוֹכֵנוּ,	הֲמוֹנִים אֲשֶׁר שָׁכְנוּ
וּפֶרֶץ בְּלִי נִגְדָּר,	חָרְבוֹת עֲזָבוּנוּ
בְּגוֹלָה וְהָיוּ חֹל	וְהָלְכוּ כָּל־יקֹדֶשׁ 5
לְשׁוֹשָׁן בְּתוֹךְ דַּרְדָּר	וְאֵיךְ תִּשְׁאֲלוּ הָדָר
דְּרוּשֵׁי אֲדֹנֵיהֶם	דְּחוּיֵי שְׁכֵנֵיהֶם
וְאִישׁ לֹא־יְהִי נֶעְדָּר	לְכֻלָּם בְּשֵׁם יִקְרָא
יְשׁוֹבֵב בָּאַחֲרֹנָה	הֲדָרָם כְּרִאשֹׁנָה
מְאוֹרָם אֲשֶׁר קָדָר:	וְיָאִיר כְּאוֹר שִׁבְעָה 10

62

WONDERFUL IS THY LOVE

(For rhymed version see page 165)

May my sweet song be pleasing in Thy sight,
    and the goodness of my praise,
O Belovèd, who art flown afar from me, at
    the evil of my deeds!
But I have held fast unto the corner of the
    garment of love of Him who is tre-
    mendous and wonderful.

Eccles. 2,10.   Enough for me is the glory of Thy name;
    that is my portion alone from all my labour.

II Sam. 1,26.   Increase the sorrow, I shall love but more,
    for wonderful is Thy love to me.

62

נפלאה אהבתך לי

אהבה

— — — ◡ — — | — — — ◡ — — ‖

שִׁירִי וּמֵיטַב מַהֲלָלִי	יִיטַב בְּעֵינֶיךָ נְעִים.
מִנִּי לְרֵעַ מַעֲלָלִי	הַדּוֹד אֲשֶׁר הִרְחִיק נָדֹד
דוּתוֹ וְהוּא נוֹרָא וּפֶלִי	וָאַחֲזַק בִּכְנַף יָדֹ־
חֶלְקִי לְבַד מִכָּל־עֲמָלִי	דִּ־ילִי כְּבוֹד שְׁמְךָ וְהוּא
כִּי נִפְלְאָה אַהֲבָתְךָ לִי!	הוֹסֵף כְּאֵב–אוֹסִיף אֱהֹב

5

63

THE DOVE AFAR

The dove, afar,[1] she flieth about the forests;
She stumbleth, she cannot shake herself free.
Flying, flitting, fluttering,
Round about her belovèd she swirleth, she
    stormeth.
She deemed a thousand years would be the
    limit of her set time,
But she is ashamed of all whereon she counted.[2]
Her Belovèd who hath afflicted her with long
    years of separation

Isa. 53,12.   Hath poured out her soul to the grave.
"Lo," she saith, "I will not make mention
    any more of His name;"

Jer. 20,9.   But it is within her heart like a burning fire.
Why wilt Thou be as an enemy to her, since
    she
Openeth wide her mouth for the rain of thy
    salvation?
And she maketh her soul believe and despaireth
    not,

Job 14,21.   Whether she win honour in His name or
    whether she be brought low.
Our God shall come and shall not keep silence;

Ps. 50,3.   All round about Him is fire; it stormeth
    exceedingly.

   [1] See the heading of Ps. 56, יונת אלם רחוקים.
   [2] The exile, to last 1000 years, should have ended in

63

יונת רחקים
על כנסת ישראל

‖‒ ◡ ‒ | ‒ ◡ ‒ | ◡ ‒ ◡ ‒

יוֹנַת רְחֹקִים נֶדְדָה יַעֲרָה

כָּשְׁלָה וְלֹא יָכְלָה לְהִתְנַעֲרָה

הִתְעוֹפְפָה, הִתְנוֹפְפָה, חוֹפֵפָה

סָבִיב לְדוֹדָה סֹחֲרָה סֹעֲרָה:

וַתַּחֲשֹׁב אֶלֶף לְקֵץ מוֹעֲדָה   5

אַךְ חָפְרָה מִכֹּל אֲשֶׁר שָׁעֲרָה:

דּוֹדָהּ אֲשֶׁר עִנָּהּ בְּאֹרֶךְ נְדֹד

שָׁנִים, וְנַפְשָׁהּ אֶל שְׁאוֹל הֶעֱרָה:

הֵן אָמְרָה לֹא־אֶזְכְּרָה עוֹד שְׁמוֹ

וַיְהִי בְתוֹךְ לִבָּהּ כְּאֵשׁ בֹּעֲרָה   10

לָמָּה כְאוֹיֵב תִּהְיֶה לָהּ, וְהִיא

פִּיהָ לְמַלְקוֹשׁ יִשְׁעֲךָ פָּעֲרָה

וַתַּאֲמִין נַפְשָׁהּ וְלֹא נוֹאָשָׁה

אִם־כֻּבְּדָה בִשְׁמוֹ וְאִם־צֹעֲרָה

יָבֹא אֱלֹהֵינוּ וְאַל־יֶחֱרַשׁ   15

עַל כָּל־סְבִיבָיו אֵשׁ מְאֹד נִשְׂעֲרָה:

64

MORNING HYMN

All the stars of morning sing to Thee,
For the radiance of their shining is of Thee;
And the sons of God, standing by the watches
Of night and day, glorify the glorious Name;
And the company of saints receive the word
    from them,
And, every dawn, wake early to seek Thine
    house.

the year 4828. If the word נדוד which occurs so obscurely
in the following line is a mnemonic, as S. D. Luzzatto
suggests, the inference is that the exile had endured 64
years over the thousand and that the poem was written
in 4892 = 1132 C. E.

64

כל כוכבי בקר

בקשה לשחרית

– – – | ∪ – | – – | ∪ – ‖

כָּל־כּוֹכְבֵי בֹקֶר לְךָ יָשִׁירוּ
כִּי־זָהֲרֵיהֶם מִמְּךָ יַזְהִירוּ
וּבְנֵי אֱלֹהִים עֹמְדִים עַל־מִשְׁמָרוֹת
לַיְל וְיוֹם שֵׁם נֶאְדָּר יַאְדִּירוּ
וּקְהַל קְדֹשִׁים קִבְּלוּ מֵהֶם, וְכָל־
שַׁחַר לְשַׁחֵר בֵּיתְךָ יָעִירוּ:

5

65

CREATURE, IMPULSE AND CREATOR

Why believe in fate wherein there is no truth?
(Ah me! my labour is great, and my day is
　　short).
Every man exhorteth his brother that he sin
　　not,
Saying, "Take heed to thyself, lest the *Yezer*[1]
　　tempt thee."
But if he himself should sin, he thinketh:
"What is there in the power of a man to
　　do?—
The creature and the *Yezer* are in the hand of
　　the Creator."

---

[1] The evil inclination. There is a play on three words
in the last line, יצור a Creature, יצר man's evil impulse,
יוצר the Creator.

65

הַיְצוּר וְהַיֵּצֶר בְּיַד הַיּוֹצֵר

‮– – ‿ – | – ‿ – | ‿ – ‿ – | ‿ – ‖‬

מַה־תַּאֲמִין בִּזְמָן אֲשֶׁר אֵין בּוֹ אֱמֶת
הָה כִּי עֲמָלִי רַב וְיוֹמִי קָצֵר
כָּל־אִישׁ יְצֵו אָחִיו לְבִלְתִּי יֶחֱטָא
לֵאמֹר שְׁמָר־לָךְ פֶּן־יְסִיתְךָ יֵצֶר
וּבְעֵת חֲטֹא שָׂח מַה־בְּיַד אִישׁ לַעֲשׂוֹת
הַיְצוּר וְהַיֵּצֶר בְּיַד הַיּוֹצֵר:

5

66

THE LORD IS MY PORTION

(For rhymed version see page 166)

Servants of time—the slaves of slaves are they;
The Lord's servant, he alone is free.
Therefore when each man seeketh his portion,
"The Lord is my portion," saith my soul.

66

חלקי אדני

‮‮- - - | - ‿ - | - ‿ - | - ‿ - ‖‬

עַבְדֵי זְמָן עַבְדֵי עֲבָדִים הֵם
עֶבֶד אֲדֹנָי הוּא לְבַד חָפְשִׁי
עַל־כֵּן בְּבַקֵּשׁ כָּל־אֱנוֹשׁ חֶלְקוֹ
חֶלְקִי אֲדֹנָי אָמְרָה נַפְשִׁי:

67

A JOY FOR EVER

In Praise of the Torah

Who is this of beauteous countenance that
    showeth like the sun,
That before men of renown covereth not her
    fairness?

Prov. 8,30. Pure unto the foster-Father who hath taken
Esther 2,7.   her to Himself for a daughter,
She is a joy for ever that groweth not old.[1]
Before kings she speaketh—she is not ashamed;
Hos. 13,8. She campeth also in the innermost heart of
    the wise.
Praising herself, she saith: "Verily my Creator
Prov. 8,22. Acquired me before all else, with His right
    hand."
To the sons of God she calleth, what time
    she hath prepared
Dan. 5,1. A table of savoury food and hath made a feast:
Gen. 49,20. "By me are royal dainties given;
By me the tongue of all the dumb singeth
    glowing words;
Prov. 8,15. By me the just of heart decree justice;
By me the eye of men in darkness seeth light;
Prov. 7,15. By me the soul that seeketh for my face
    findeth sweetness,
By me she cleareth every crookedness from
    off her path;

[1] Compare the opening lines of Keats' "Endymion."

67

עֲדִנָה עֲדִי־עַד

בשבח התורה

‒ ‒ ‒ | ‒ ∪ ‒ ‒ | ‒ ∪ ‒ ‒ | ‒ ‒ ▯

מִי זֹאת הֲדַר פָּנִים כְּשֶׁמֶשׁ גָּלְתָה

יָפְיָה פְּנֵי אַנְשֵׁי יְקָר לֹא כִסְּתָה

בָּרָה לְאִמָּן שֶׁלְּקָחָה לוֹ לְבַת

עֶדְנָה עֲדִי־עַד לָהּ אֲשֶׁר לֹא בָלְתָה

לִפְנֵי מְלָכִים דִּבְּרָה לֹא נִכְלְמָה   5

גַּם תּוֹךְ סְגוֹר לֵב הַחֲכָמִים חֲנָתָה

מִתְהַלָּלָה לֵאמֹר בְּאָמְנָם יְצָרִי

אֹתִי בְּטֶרֶם כֹּל יְמִינוֹ קָנָתָה

לִבְנֵי אֱלֹהִים קָרְאָה אֵת עָרְכָה

שֻׁלְחָן בְּמַטְעַמִּים וְלָחֶם עָשָׂתָה   10

בִּי מַעֲדַנֵּי הַמְּלָכִים נִתְּנוּ

בִּי כָל־לְשׁוֹן אִלֵּם בְּצַחוֹת עָנָתָה

בִּי חָקְקוּ צֶדֶק בְּלִבָּם צָדְקוּ

בִּי עֵין מְתֵי חֹשֶׁךְ מְאוֹרִים רָאָתָה

בִּי נָעֲמָה נֶפֶשׁ לְפָנַי שְׁחָרָה   15

בִּי כָל־עֲקַלְקַלּוֹת נְתִיבָה פִּנְּתָה

By me the foot of them that seek me is held
 up from slipping;
By me the hand of them that love me mounteth
 up above the wealthy.
Mine is strength and mine is glory and mine
 a robe of honour;
Mine is light like a sun that waneth not
 towards evening.
Mine are the searchings out of counsel which
 cannot be likened to fine gold;
Mine dignity and royalty, befitting them that
 take hold on me;
Mine are the precious things, laid up for the
 upright;
Mine is the step to the fortress, built for a
 stronghold.

Jer. 18,15. Unto me they that walk upon the highway
 bow them down;

Ps. 84,3. For me the soul longeth, yea even fainteth.

Ps. 127,2. Come ye, and eat not the bread of sorrows,
Turn into the garden that hath drunk its
 fill of the glory of God.
Let not your heart incline after the helpers

Job 9,13. Of Rahab, when these run whither they be
 not bidden.

Cant. 1,8. By the shepherds' tents and their footprints,
 feed your flocks;
Then will ye know that your foot hath never
 strayed."

This is she whom they that know her have not
 concealed;
From age to age hath she been an heritage in
 their hand.

בִּי נִסְעֲדָה רֶגֶל מְבַקְשֵׁי מִדְחוֹת
בִּי יַד מְאַהֲבַי עַל־עֲשִׁירִים עָלָתָה
לִי אוֹן וְלִי כָבוֹד וְלִי אֶדֶר יָקָר
לִי אוֹר כְּשָׁמֶשׁ לַעֲרוֹב לֹא פֶנְתָה   20
לִי מָחְקְרֵי עֵצוֹת וְלֹא שָׁוֶה בְּפָז
לִי הוֹד וּמַמְלָכָה לְתֹפְשֵׂי יָאָתָה
לִי מַחֲמַדִּים לַיְשָׁרִים נִצְפָּנוּ
לִי מַעֲלַת מָעוֹז לְמִבְצָר נִבְנָתָה
לִי הֹלְכֵי דָרֶךְ סְלוּלָה שָׁחֲחוּ   25
לִי הַנְּשָׁמָה נִכְסְפָה גַם־כֵּלְתָה
בֹּאוּ וְאֶל לָחֶם עֲצָבִים תִּלָּחֲמוּ
סוּרוּ לְנָוֶה מִכְּבוֹד אֵל רֶוָתָה
אַל־יַט לְבַבְכֶם אַחֲרֵי הָעֹזְרִים
רַהַב בְּרוּצָם לַאֲשֶׁר לֹא צֻוָּתָה   30
עַל־מִשְׁכְּנוֹת רֹעִים וְעִקְבוֹתָם רְעוּ
תֵּדְעוּ אֲזַי כִּי רַגְלְכֶם לֹא נָטָתָה
זֹאת הִיא אֲשֶׁר לֹא כַחֲדוּהָ יֹדְעִים
מִדּוֹר לְדוֹר נַחֲלָה בְּיָדָם הָיָתָה

Jer. 48,11.   Her perfume is not changed; as at this day,
             so was it ever:
           She retaineth the same fair form, she groweth
             not dim.
           Refrain, ye men, from being like foxes
           Whose way is contrary to the king and his
             law;
           Cease from being head over them that from the
             law stray far,

Ezek. 19,2.   And be a tail[1] to the lions' whelps which she
             hath reared,
           Which eat her bread in order to fight them
             that wage war on her,[2]
           That would do, every man, as his soul desireth,
           Every man of whom goeth his own way, for
             in truth,

Jer. 31,28-29. The tooth that eateth sour grapes, that alone

Ezek. 18,2.   is set on edge.
           But as for me, I will cleave to her, and my
             soul shall hold fast
           To her cords, and because of her it waiteth
             for the Lord.

Gen. 12,13.   Truly she is my sister, and sheddeth sweetness
             upon me,
           The while I take pleasure in her, and she in me.
           I have gloried all my life-long that she is my
             sister,

Gen. 12,13.   And my soul liveth for her sake.

---

[1] See Ethics of the Fathers IV, 20.

[2] Note play on the word לחם.

רֵיחָהּ בְּלִי נָמַר כְּזֶה הַיּוֹם כְּאָז 35

תָּמִיד בְּעֵינֶיהָ עֲמָדָה לֹא כָהֲתָה

עָזְבָה אֱנוֹשׁ מִהְיוֹת כְּשׁוּעָלִים אֲשֶׁר

דַּרְכָּם עֲלֵי־מֶלֶךְ וְדָתוֹ עִוְּתָה

חָדְלָה הֱיוֹתָךְ עַל־רַחֲקִי דָת לְרֹאשׁ

וְהָיָה זְנַב גּוּרֵי אֲרָיוֹת רִבְתָה 40

הַלֹּחֲמִים לַחֲמָה לְלַחֵם לֹחֲמִים

לָהּ, לַעֲשׂוֹת כָּל־אִישׁ כְּנַפְשׁוֹ אִוְּתָה

כָּל־אִישׁ בְּדַרְכּוֹ יַהֲלֹךְ לוֹ כִּי אֱמֶת

שֵׁן אָכְלָה בׂשֶׂר לְבַדָּהּ קָהֲתָה

וַאֲנִי בְּזֹאת אַחֲזִיק וְחֶבְלָה תֶּאֱחֹז 45

נַפְשִׁי וְעָקֵב זֹאת אֲדֹנָי קִוְּתָה

אָמְנָם אֲחוֹתִי הִיא וְעָלַי נָעֱמָה

עֵת בָּהּ אֲנִי אֶרְצֶה וְהִיא בִּי רָצְתָה

אֶתְהַלֲלָה מִדֵּי הֱיוֹתִי כִּי אֲחוֹ־

תִי הִיא וְנַפְשִׁי בַּעֲבוּרָהּ חָיָתָה: 50

68

THE BRIDE THAT LONGETH FOR THEE

She goeth out to meet Thee—the bride that
    longeth for Thee.
Since the day she could no more supplicate
    in Thy sanctuary, she hath pined for Thee.
She is abashed each time she would be going
    up to the holy mount,
For she seeth that strangers go up, but not
    she.
And she standeth afar off, worshipping toward
Thy Temple from every place whither she is
    exiled.
The words of her entreaty she sendeth, an
    offering to Thee,
While she hangeth her heart and her eyes
    upon Thy throne.
Look Thou and listen and hear her cry:
She is calling in the bitterness of her heart and
    her fainting soul.

Ps. 84,3.

68

כלה לך כלתה
רשות לשמחת תורה

‏—ᴗ—|—ᴗ—|—ᴗ—‖—ᴗ—

יָצְאָה לְקַדְּמָךְ כַּלָּה לָךְ כָּלָתָה
מִיּוֹם אֲשֶׁר לֹא חִלָּתָה קָדְשָׁךְ חָלָתָה

הִשְׁתּוֹמֲמָה מִדֵּי עֲלָתָה לְהַר קֹדֶשׁ
כִּי־רָאֲתָה זָרִים עָלוּ וְלֹא עָלָתָה

וַתַּעֲמֹד רָחוֹק מִשְׁתַּחֲוָה נֹכַח
הֵיכָלֵךְ מִכָּל־מָקוֹם אֲשֶׁר גָּלָתָה

דִּבְרֵי תְחִנָּתָהּ שָׁלָחָה לָךְ מִנְחָה
לִבָּהּ וְעֵינֶיהָ מוּל כִּסְאֲךָ תָּלָתָה

הַשְׁקֵף וְהַאֲזִינָה וּשְׁמַע לְשַׁוְעָתָהּ
קָרְאָה בְּמַר לִבָּהּ וְנַפְשָׁהּ אֲשֶׁר כָּלָתָה:

5

10

69

UNTIL DAY AND NIGHT SHALL CEASE

(For rhymed version see page 167)

The sun and moon, these minister for ever;
The laws of day and night come never to an end.
Given as signs are they to Jacob's seed,
That they shall ever be a nation, that they
    shall not be cut off.
If with the left hand He should thrust them
    off, with the right hand doth He draw
    them nigh.
Let them not say, " 'Tis desperate ", at the
    time of their ruin;
Let them only believe they are eternal, and
    that
They shall not cease until day and night shall
    cease.

69

עד יום וליל ישבתו

‒ ‒ | ‒ ∪ ‒ | ‒ ‒ | ‒ ∪ ‒ ‖

שֶׁמֶשׁ וְיָרֵחַ לְעוֹלָם שֵׁרְתוּ

חֻקּוֹת בְּיוֹם וָלַיְלָה לֹא נִצְמָתוּ

הֵם נִתְּנוּ אֹתוֹת לְזֶרַע יַעֲקֹב

לִהְיוֹת לְעוֹלָם גּוֹי וְלֹא יִכָּרֵתוּ

אִם בַּשְׂמֹאל דּוֹחָם בְּיָמִין קֵרְבָם   5

אַל יֹאמְרוּ נוֹאָשׁ בְּעֵת יִתְעַנּוּתוּ

אַךְ יַאֲמִינוּ כִּי לְעוֹלָם הֵם וְכִי

לֹא יִשָּׁבְתוּ עַד יוֹם וָלַיְל יִשָּׁבְתוּ׃

70

O GOD, THY NAME

O God, Thy name! I will exalt Thee, and
     Thy righteousness I will not conceal.
I have given ear, and I have trusted; I will
     not question, I will not prove:
For how should a vessel of clay say unto its
     moulder, What doest Thou?
I have sought Him, I have met Him—a tower
     of strength, a rock of trust—
The radiant one, like shining light, unveiled,
     uncovered!

Praised be He and glorified, exalted and extolled!

The beauty of Thy glory and the strength
     of Thy hand the heavens declare,
When they dawn and when they wane and
     when they bow their faces;
And angels walk amid the stones of fire and
     water.
Isa. 57.19.   They testify to Thee, they thank Thee, Who
     createst the fruit of the lips,
For Thou upholdest, and failest not—without
     arms, without hands—
The depths and the heights, the Beings and
     the Throne.

Praised be He and glorified, exalted and extolled!

70

יה שמך ארוממך

רשות לקדיש

— — | — — —

יָהּ שִׁמְךָ   אֲרוֹמִמְךָ   וְצִדְקָתְךָ   לֹא־אֲכַסֶּה
הֶאֱזַנְתִּי   וְהֶאֱמַנְתִּי   לֹא־אֶשְׁאַל   וְלֹא־אֲנַסֶּה
וְאֵיךְ יֹאמַר   כְּלִי חֹמֶר   אֵלַי יִצְרוֹ   מַה־תַּעֲשֶׂה
דְּרַשְׁתִּיהוּ   פְּגַשְׁתִּיהוּ   לְמִגְדָּל־עֹז   וְצוּר מַחְסֶה
5 הַבָּהִיר   כְּאוֹר מַזְהִיר   בְּלִי מָסָךְ   וְלֹא מְכַסֶּה
יִשְׁתַּבַּח   וְיִתְפָּאַר   וְיִתְרוֹמֵם   וְיִתְנַשֵּׂא:

הָדַר כְּבוֹדְךָ   וְעֹז יָדְךָ   מְסַפְּרִים הֵד   שָׁמָיִם
בְּעֵת עֲלוֹתָם   וְעֵת פְּנוֹתָם   וְעֵת שְׁחוֹתָם   אַפַּיִם
וּמַלְאָכִים   נֶהֱלָכִים   בְּתוֹךְ אַבְנֵי   אֵשׁ וּמָיִם
10 יְעִידוּךָ   וְיוֹדוּךָ   בּוֹרֵא נִיב   שְׂפָתָיִם
כִּי תִסְבֹּל   וְלֹא תִבֹּל   בְּלִי זְרוֹעַ   וְיָדַיִם
תַּחְתִּיּוֹת   וְעֶלְיוֹת   וְהַחַיּוֹת   וְהַכִּסֵּא
יִשְׁתַּבַּח   וְיִתְפָּאַר   וְיִתְרוֹמֵם   וְיִתְנַשֵּׂא:

And who can utter the glory of Him who
    formed the clouds by His word?
He liveth eternally, albeit hidden; in the
    highest heights His abode.
And in His love for the son of His house,
    within his tent He set His presence,
And granted vision to prophecy, to look
    toward His likeness.
And there is no form and no measurement,
    and no end to the knowledge of Him;
Only the vision of Him in the sight of
    His prophets is like a King high and
    exalted.[1]

Praised be He and glorified, exalted and extolled!

The tale of mighty acts is beyond telling, and
    who can declare His praises?
Happy is the man who is quick to perceive
    the strength of His great deeds,
And stayeth himself upon God who upholdeth
    the universe in His arms,
Ezek. 1.14.   And proclaimeth His awe whate'er betide,
    and holdeth just His acts,
And giveth thanks for all He doeth, since for
    His own sake are His doings,
And since a terrible day of God cometh when
    there shall be judgment for all work.

Praised be He and glorified, exalted and extolled!

[1] The text is possibly defective here. The line is
unlikely to have ended with a word giving practically the
same sense as the last one of the refrain. See the last
word in all the other verses.

וּמִי יְמַלֵּל　כְּבוֹד מְחֹלַל שְׁחָקִים בְּ־　אֲמִירָתוֹ

חַי עוֹלָם　אֲשֶׁר נָעְלָם　בְּגָבְהֵי רוֹם　מְעוֹנָתוֹ

15 וּבִרְצֹתוֹ　בְּבָן־בֵּיתוֹ　בְּאָהֳלוֹ שָׁת　שְׁכִינָתוֹ

וְשָׁם מַרְאוֹת　לַנְּבוּאוֹת　לְהַבִּיט אֶל־　תְּמוּנָתוֹ

וְאֵין תַּבְנִית　וְאֵין תָּכְנִית　וְאֵין קֵץ לְ־　תְּבוּנָתוֹ

רַק מַרְאָיו　בְּעֵין נְבִיאָיו　כְּמֶלֶךְ רָם　וּמִתְנַשֵּׂא

יִשְׁתַּבַּח　וְיִתְפָּאַר　וְיִתְרוֹמֵם　וְיִתְנַשֵּׂא:

דְּבַר גְּבוּרוֹת בְּלִי סְפֹרוֹת　וּמִי יְסַפֵּר　תְּהִלּוֹתָיו

20 אַשְׁרֵי אִישׁ　אֲשֶׁר יָחִישׁ　לְהַכִּיר עֹז　גְּדֻלּוֹתָיו

וְיִסָּמֵךְ　בְּאֵל תֹּמֵךְ　עוֹלָם עַל־　זְרוֹעוֹתָיו

וְיַעֲרִיצוּ　שׁוֹב וְרָצוֹא　וְיַצְדִּיק דִּין　עֲלִילוֹתָיו

וְיוֹדֶה עַל　אֲשֶׁר פָּעַל　כִּי לְמַעֲנוּ　פְּעֻלּוֹתָיו

וְכִי יֶשׁ־יוֹם　לְאֵל אָיֹם　וְדִין עַל־כָּל־　הַמַּעֲשֶׂה

יִשְׁתַּבַּח　וְיִתְפָּאַר　וְיִתְרוֹמֵם　וְיִתְנַשֵּׂא:

Consider deeply and prepare thyself and re-
 flect on thine own secret,
And examine what thou art and whence thine
 origin,
Who set thee up, who gave thee understanding,
 whose power moveth thee;
And look unto the mighty acts of God and
 waken the glory in thee.
Search out His works, only upon Himself
Job 1,12.   put not forth thine hand
Ben Sira 3,21-22. When thou seekest the end and the beginning,
Ḥagigah 13a.   the too wonderful, the deeply hid.

Praised be He and glorified, exalted and extolled!

25 הַשְׁתּוֹנֵן וְהַכּוֹנֵן וְהִתְבּוֹנֵן בְּסוֹדֶךָ

וְהַבֵּטָה מָה אַתָּה וּמֵאַיִן יְסוֹדֶךָ

וּמִי הֱכִינֶךָ וְכֹחַ מִי יְנִידֶךָ

וְהַבֵּט אֶל גְּבוּרוֹת אֵל וְהָעִירָה כְּבוֹדֶךָ

חֲקֹר פְּעָלָיו רַק אֵלָיו אַל־תִּשְׁלַח יָדֶךָ

30 כִּי תִדְרֹשׁ בְּסוֹף וּבְרֹאשׁ בַּמִּפְלָא וּבַמְכֻסֶּה

יִשְׁתַּבַּח וְיִתְפָּאַר וְיִתְרוֹמֵם וְיִתְנַשֵּׂא:

71

THOUGH I SIT IN DARKNESS

O silent Dove,[1] pour out thy whispered prayer,

Ps. 120,5. Stricken amid the tents of Meshekh;
And lift up thy soul unto God—
Thy banner, thy chariot and thy horseman—
Who kindleth the light of thy sun:
Isa. 45,7.   *Who formeth light and createth darkness.*

To the Whole He called with His word,
And it arose in a moment, at His bidding,
To show unto all the strength of His glory
In the world which, no longer void, He had
          formed,
What time, from the east, unto His light
Ex. 10,21.   *He called and moved the darkness.*

And the host of His heavens heard
The word: "Let there be Light"; and it
          was known
That there is a Rock by whom are cleft

    [1] See heading of Ps. 56.

71

כי אשב בחשך

יוצר

————————

יוֹנַת אֵלֶם צְקִי לַחֲשֵׁךְ
הֲלוּמָה בְּתוֹךְ מִשְׁכְּנֵי־מָשֵׁךְ
וּשְׂאִי לֶאֱלוֹהַּ נַפְשֵׁךְ
דְּגַלֵּךְ רִכְבֵּךְ וּפָרָשֵׁךְ
הַמַּזְרִיחַ אוֹר שִׁמְשֵׁךְ   5
יוֹצֵר אוֹר וּבוֹרֵא חֹשֶׁךְ:

לַכֹּל קָרָא בְּמַאֲמָרוֹ
וְעָמַד רֶגַע לְפִי דְבָרוֹ
לְהַרְאוֹת לַכֹּל עֹז יְקָרוֹ
בְּעוֹלָם לֹא־תֹהוּ יְצָרוֹ   10
עֵת מִמִּזְרָח לְאוֹרוֹ
קָרָא, וַיָּמָשׁ חֹשֶׁךְ:

וּצְבָא שְׁחָקִיו שָׁמָעוּ
אָמַר יְהִי אוֹר, וְנוֹדָעוּ
כִּי יֵשׁ צוּר, בּוֹ נִבְקָעוּ   15

Job 38,6. The clouds, and the corner-stones laid.
And they gave thanks to their Maker, since
they knew
Ecc. 2,13. *The excellency of light over darkness.*

So will He yet light up my gloom,
And uphold him who raiseth my fallen estate,
And make the light of mine assembly shine
forth.
Then the chosen one yet shall boast herself:
"Behold the light of the Rock of my praise
Micah 7,8. *Is mine, though I sit in darkness*"[1]

[1] In the acrostic יהודה לוי the customary ה of הלוי is
missing.

שְׁחָקִים, וּפִנּוֹת הָטְבָּעוּ
וְהוֹדוּ לְיוֹצְרָם וְיָדָעוּ
יִתְרוֹן אוֹר מִן־הַחשֶׁךְ:

יָאִיר כֵּן עוֹד אֲפֵלָתִי
וְיִסְמוֹךְ לְקוֹמֵם נְפִילָתִי
וְיַזְרִיחַ אוֹר קְהִלָּתִי
וְתִתְהַלֵּל עוֹד סְגֻלָּתִי
הִנֵּה אוֹר צוּר תְּהִלָּתִי
לִי, כִּי־אֵשֵׁב בַּחשֶׁךְ:

20

72

NOW COMETH THE LIGHT

Ps. 76,5.   Together in Thy light, O God resplendent,
Ps. 36,10.   *Do we see light!*

Isa. 9, 1.   The people that walked in darkness—
           Their hope[1] how long deferred!—
Gen. 49,17,19.   While biting sin still troopeth at their heel,
Isa. 18,4.   Upon them, like clear heat in sunshine,
Job 38,19.   *Shall dwell the light.*

           With veil on the uncovered head,
           With glory in place of rent apparel,
Ps. 97,11.   Wilt Thou clothe them; the light, once sown,
                make manifest
           Again, as Thou hast said: "Let there be light,
Gen. 1,3.   *And there was light."*

           Thy banner, over them whose knees stumble,
           Upraise, and clear the way before them
Malachi 3,1.   By an Angel; and Thou wilt bless
           The seed of the upright, what time Thou
                makest light[2]
Job 24,13.   *Of them that rebel against the light.*

[1] I have followed S. D. Luzzatto and Brody in their pointing of שִׂבְרוֹ "his hope", although שֶׁבְרוֹ is also possible in the sense of long drawn out calamity.

[2] This is an attempt to reproduce the play on words continually taking place in the Hebrew rhymes.

72

כי בא אור

מאורה

‗ ‗ ‗ ‗|‗ ‗ ‗ ‗ ⌣ ‗ ‗
‗ ‗ ‗ ‗ ‗ ‗

נִרְאָה־אוֹר: יַחַד בְּאוֹרֶךָ אֵל נֵאוֹר

                                    הָעָם אֲשֶׁר הָלַךְ חֹשֶׁךְ

                                    שֹׁבְרוֹ עֲדֵי־אָן יִמְשַׁךְ

                                    יָגוּד עֲקֵבוֹ חֵטְא נִשֵׁךְ

יִשְׁכָּן־אוֹר: 5 עָלָיו כְּחֹם צַח עֲלֵי־אוֹר

                                    וּצְנִיף עֲלֵי־רֹאשׁ פָּרוּעַ

                                    וְיָקָר מְקוֹם סוּת קָרוּעַ

                                    תַּלְבֵּשׁ, וְגַל אוֹר זָרוּעַ

וַיְהִי־אוֹר: שֵׁנִית, כְּמַאְמָרְךָ יְהִי אוֹר

                     10 דִּגְלָךְ עֲלֵי כֹשְׁלַי בָּרֵךְ

                                    הָרֵם, וְלִפְנֵיהֶם דָּרֵךְ

                                    פְּנֵה בְמַלְאָךְ, וּתְבָרֵךְ

מֹרְדֵי־אוֹר: זֶרַע יְשָׁרִים, יוֹם תָּאוֹר

Job 7,2.
　　　While he moaneth like a servant panting after
　　　　　the shade,
　　　Do Thou lay the majesty of Thy salvation
　　　　　upon him;
　　　And cry: "How long, O sluggard,

Prov. 6,9.
　　　Wilt thou sleep in the house of darkness?
　　　　　Arise, shine!

Isa. 60,1.
　　　　Now cometh the light!"

Zech. 4,7.
　　　"Grace, grace," proclaim; and set up two rows
Zech.4,3,11–14.
　　　Of olive trees for kindling the lights,
　　　And they shall serve for lamps—
　　　Their oil within the shrine of God resplendent,
　　　　For the Light![1]

---

[1] This verse may possibly be an interpolation to adapt
the poem to Hanukah. The acrostic חזק in addition to
יהודה is rare with this poet.

הוֹמָה כְּעֶבֶד יִשְׁאַף צֵל

הוֹד יִשְׁעֲךָ עָלָיו הַאֲצֵל   15

וּקְרָא עֲדֵי מָתַי עָצֵל

כִּי־בָא אוֹר: תִּשְׁכַּב בְּבֵית חֹשֶׁךְ? קוּם אוֹר

חָן חֵן קְרָא, וּשְׁתֵּי שׁוּרוֹת

זֵתִים לְהָאִיר הַנֵּרוֹת

קוֹמֵם, וְהָיוּ לִמְאוֹרוֹת

לַמָּאוֹר: שַׁמְנָם בְּמִקְדַּשׁ אֵל נָאוֹר   20

73

GOD IN ALL

(For rhymed version see page 168)

Lord, where shall I find Thee?
High and hidden is Thy place;
And where shall I not find Thee?
The world is full of Thy glory.

Found in the innermost being,
He set up the ends of the earth:
The refuge for the near,
The trust for those far off.
Thou dwellest amid the Cherubim,
Thou abidest in the clouds;
Thou art praised by Thine hosts
Yet art raised above their praise.
The whirling worlds cannot contain Thee;
How then the chambers of a temple?

And though Thou be uplifted over them
Upon a throne high and exalted,
Yet art Thou near to them,
Of their very spirit and their flesh.
Their own mouth testifieth for them
That Thou alone art their Creator.
Who shall not fear Thee
Since the yoke of Thy kingdom is their yoke?
Or who shall not call to Thee
Since Thou givest them their food?

I have sought Thy nearness,
With all my heart have I called Thee,

73

כבודך מלא עולם
אופן לשמחת תורה

‫— — — — — ‬ | ‫— — — — —‬

יָהּ אָנָה אֶמְצָאֶךָ   מְקוֹמְךָ נַעֲלָה וְנֶעְלָם

וְאָנָה לֹא אֶמְצָאֶךָ   כְּבוֹדְךָ מָלֵא עוֹלָם:

הַנִּמְצָא בַּקְּרָבִים   אַפְסֵי־אָרֶץ הֵקִים

הַמִּשְׂגָּב לַקְּרֵבִים   הַמִּבְטָח לָרְחֹקִים

אַתָּה יֹשֵׁב כְּרוּבִים   אַתָּה שֹׁכֵן שְׁחָקִים   5

תִּתְהַלֵּל בִּצְבָאֶךָ   וְאַתָּ עַל־רֹאשׁ מַהֲלָלָם

נֻגַּל לֹא־יְשָׂאֶךָ   אַף כִּי־חַדְרֵי אוּלָם:

וּבְהִנָּשְׂאֲךָ עֲלֵיהֶם   עַל־כֵּס נִשָּׂא וָרָם

אַתָּה קָרוֹב אֲלֵיהֶם   מֵרוּחָם וּמִבְּשָׂרָם

פִּיהֶם יָעִיד בָּהֶם   כִּי־אֵין בִּלְתְּךָ יְצָרָם   10

מִי זֶה לֹא יָרַאֲךָ   וְעַל מַלְכוּתְךָ עָלָם

אוֹ מִי לֹא יִקְרָאֶךָ   וְאַתָּה נוֹתֵן אָכְלָם:

דָּרַשְׁתִּי קֻרְבָתְךָ   בְּכָל־לִבִּי קְרָאתִיךָ

And going out to meet Thee
I found Thee coming toward me,
Even as, in the wonder of Thy might,
In the sanctuary I have beheld Thee.
Who shall say he hath not seen Thee?—
Lo, the heavens and their hosts
Declare the fear of Thee
Though their voice be not heard.

Doth then, in very truth,
God dwell with man?
What can he think—every one that thinketh,
Whose foundation is in the dust—
Since Thou art holy, dwelling
Amid their praises and their glory?
Angels adore Thy wonder,
Standing in the everlasting height;
Over their heads is Thy throne,
And Thou upholdest them all!

לִקְרָאתִי מְצָאתִיךָ   וּבְצֵאתִי לִקְרָאתְךָ

בַּקֹּדֶשׁ חֲזִיתִיךָ   וּבְפִלְאֵי גְבוּרָתְךָ   15

הֵן שָׁמַיִם וְחֵילָם   מִי יֹאמַר לֹא־רָאָךְ

בְּלִי נִשְׁמַע קוֹלָם: יַגִּידוּ מוֹרָאָךְ

אֱלֹהִים אֶת־הָאָדָם   הַאָמְנָם כִּי־יֵשֵׁב

אֲשֶׁר בֶּעָפָר יְסוֹדָם   וּמַה־יַּחְשֹׁב כָּל־הֹשֵׁב

תְּהִלּוֹתָם וּכְבוֹדָם   וְאַתָּה קָדוֹשׁ יוֹשֵׁב   20

הָעֹמְדוֹת בְּרוּם עוֹלָם   חַיּוֹת יוֹדוּ פִּלְאָךְ

וְאַתָּה נֹשֵׂא כֻלָּם: עַל־רָאשֵׁיהֶם כִּסְאָךְ

74

ELIJAH AND ELISHAH

Our portents linger—
Where is the God of Elijah?[1]

The son who hearkeneth unto His words,
Crying of violence out of his sorrows,
Saith, Where is the Rock and His Names?[2]
A thousand years He hath not answered him.[3]

The Tishbite decreed for Ephraim,
And closed up the heavens;
At his word came fire and water down;
I Kings 18.   On Mount Carmel—there he proved Him.

I Kings17,10-16. He spake of the jar and the cruse,
And therein set a blessing flowering;
I Kings17,17-24. He restored the dead from the pit—
Who hath heard such things and who hath
      seen them?

II Kings 1,9-14. He caused the burning of the captains and
      their fifties;
He fasted forty days with their nights;

[1] See Mal. 3,23.
[2] Another rendering may possibly be שנותי for שמותי.
See Ps. 61,7.
[3] Jehudah Halevi lived about 1000 years after the
destruction.

74

איה אלהי אליהו
הבדלה

- - - -

אָ‎תוֹתֵינוּ הִתְמַהְמָהוּ

אַיֵּה אֱלֹהֵי אֵלִיָּהוּ

בֶּן שְׁמַע אֶל־אִמְרוֹתָיו

צָעַק חָמָס מִצָּרוֹתָיו

אָמַר אַיֵּה צוּר וּשְׁמוֹתָיו   5

אֶלֶף שָׁנִים לֹא עָנָהוּ.

גָּזַר תִּשְׁבִּי עַל־אֶפְרַיִם

וַיַּעְצֹר אֶת־הַשָּׁמַיִם

וְעַל־פִּיו יָרְדוּ אֵשׁ וָמַיִם

הַר הַכַּרְמֶל שָׁם נִסָּהוּ.   10

דִּבֶּר עַל־כַּד עִם־צַפַּחַת

וּבְרָכָה שָׁם בָּם פָּרַחַת

הֵשִׁיב הַמֵּת מִן־הַשַּׁחַת

מִי־שָׁמַע זֶה, וּמִי רָאָהוּ

הִבְעִיר שָׂרִים וַחֲמִשֵּׁיהֶם   15

צָם אַרְבָּעִים עִם־אֲמִשֵּׁיהֶם

I Kings 17,4-6. The ravens assembled as though called together
To give him his food.

And when he went up on high in a whirlwind,
And in a burning chariot of fire,
II Kings 2,12 Then turned Elisha, bitterly crying:
"My father, my father!"   but he answered
  him not.

Job 38,30.   The floods of Jordan were congealed,
II Sam. 22,37. So that their feet slipped not;
Ps. 18,37.   Also for Elisha stood they up—
They that looked on him saw and were amazed.

Those watching for the signs foretold—
How long, until they see the wondrous
    happenings
When these marvels are wrought before them,
The work of the Lord which is terrible.[1]

---

[1] The alphabet in acrostic reaches only to the letter ח.

נוֹסְדוּ עָרְבִים לִמְבַקְשֵׁיהָם

לָתֵת לַחְמוֹ, וַיָּנֻהוּ.

וּבְעֵת עָלָה רוֹם בִּסְעָרָה

וּבְמִרְכֶּבֶת אֵשׁ בֹּעֲרָה 20

וֶאֱלִישָׁע שָׁב צָעַק מָרָה

אָבִי אָבִי, וְלֹא עָנָהוּ.

זִרְמֵי יַרְדֵּן הִתְלַכָּדוּ

עַד קַרְסֻלָּיו לֹא מָעָדוּ

גַּם לֶאֱלִישָׁע כֵּן עָמָדוּ 25

צֹפָיו רָאוּ וַיִּתְמָהוּ.

חוֹכֵי אֹתוֹת הַנְּבָאוֹת

מָתַי יֶחֱזוּ הַנּוֹרָאוֹת

בַּעֲשׂוֹת נֶגְדָּם הַנִּפְלָאוֹת

מַעֲשֵׂה יְיָ כִּי־נוֹרָא הוּא. 30

75

MY HEART SEETH THEE

My thoughts awaken me with Thy name,
And set Thy mercies before me.

They teach me of the soul Thou hast formed,
Bound up within me;—it is wonderful in mine
    eyes!

And my heart seeth Thee and hath faith in
    Thee
As though it had stood by at Sinai.

I have sought Thee in my visions, and there
    passed
Thy glory by me, descending in my clouds.

My musings have roused me from my couch
To bless Thy glorious Name, O Lord.

75

ולבי ראך

רשות

— ‖ ⌣ — | — ⌣ — | — ‖ — | — — ⌣

יְעִירוּנִי בְשִׁמְךָ רַעְיוֹנָי
וְיָשִׂימוּ חֲסָדֶיךָ לְפָנָי

הֲבִינוּנִי דְבַר נֶפֶשׁ יְצַרְתָּהּ
קְשׁוּרָה בִי וְהִיא נִפְלָאת בְּעֵינָי

וְלִבִּי רָאֲךָ וַיַּאֲמֶן בָּךְ
כְּאִלּוּ מַעֲמָד הָיָה בְסִינָי

5

דְרַשְׁתִּיךָ בְחֶזְיוֹנַי וְעָבַר
כְּבוֹדְךָ בִי וְיָרַד בַּעֲנָנָי

הֲקִימוּנִי שְׂעִפַּי מִיְצוּעַי
לְבָרֵךְ שֵׁם כְּבוֹדְךָ אֲדֹנָי:

10

76

A NEW SONG

(For rhymed version see page 170)

The day the depths were turned into dry land,
A new song sang the redeemed.
That day Thou wast honoured of the foe, and
    wast precious unto me,
And didst lay for Thyself a foundation of
    strength from the mouths of sucklings.[1]

Thou didst sink in deceit the feet of the
    daughter of the Anamim[2],
Cant. 7,1-2. But the steps of the Shulamite were beautiful
    in sandals.

And all that see me shall sing, when they
    look upon mine honour:[3]
Deut. 32,31. "There is none like the God of Jeshurun"—even
    though our foes be the judges.

So wilt Thou raise my banners over those that
    are left,
And gather them that are scattered as though
    gathering ears of corn.

   [1] This stanza is omitted in Heidenheim's Maḥzor,
the opening ' being taken as the first letter of the acrostic.
Brody opens the acrostic with the second '.

   [2] Mentioned among the sons of Mizraim. See Gen.10,13.

   [3] Thus Brody's reading; וכל רואי ישירון בעת הודי ישורון;
Heidenheim reads: וכל רואי ישורון בבית הודי ישוררון, which
seems less probable. (See rhymed version).

76

שירה חדשה
גאולה לפסח

— — — — | — — — —

נֶהֶפְכוּ מְצוּלִים   יוֹם לַיַבָּשָׁה

שִׁבְּחוּ גְאוּלִים: שִׁירָה חֲדָשָׁה

וְאֵלַי נֶחְמַדְתָּ   יוֹם בְּצֵר נִכְבַּדְתָּ

מִפִּי עוֹלָלִים: וְלָךְ עֹז יִסַּדְתָּ

רַגְלֵי בַת־עֲנָמִית   הִטְבַּעְתָּ בְתַרְמִית   **5**

יָפוּ בַנְּעָלִים: וּפַעֲמֵי שׁוּלַמִּית

בְּעֵת הוֹדִי יְשׁוּרוּן   וְכָל־רֹאַי יְשִׁירוּן

וְאוֹיְבֵינוּ פְּלִילִים: אֵין כָּאֵל יְשֻׁרוּן

עַל־הַנִּשְׁאָרִים   דְּנָלַי כֵּן תָּרִים

כִּמְלַקֵּט שִׁבֳּלִים: וּתְלַקֵּט פְּזוּרִים   **10**

They that come unto Thee within the covenant
    of Thy seal,
They that from the birth are consecrated to
    Thy name—

They show[1] their sign unto all that see them,
And on the corners of their garment they make
    fringes.

For whom is this one inscribed?   Discern now
    the truth:
Gen. 38,25.   Whose are the signet and the threads of blue?—

Ah, turn again to consecrate her, and cast her
    out no more;
Cant. 2,17.   And let the light of her sun arise, and the
    shadows flee away.

The belovèd exalt Thee; with song they come
    before thee:
Ex. 15,11.   "Who is like unto Thee, O Lord, among the
    mighty?"

---

[1] Brody: הַרְאוּ;   Heidenheim reads הַרְאָה. (See rhymed
version).

בִּבְרִית חֹתָמְךָ   הַבָּאִים עִמְּךָ
הֵם נֶחֱמָלִים: וּמִבָּטָן לְשִׁמְךָ

לְכָל־רֹאֶה אוֹתָם   הֵרָאוּ אֹתָם
יַעֲשׂוּ גְדִלִים: וְעַל־כַּנְפֵי כְסוּתָם

הֲכָרְנָא דְּבַר אֱמֶת   15 לְמִי זֹאת נִרְשָׁמֶת
וְהַפְּתִילִים: לְמִי הַחֹתָמֶת

וְאַל־תּוֹסֶף לְגָרְשָׁהּ   וְשׁוּב שֵׁנִית לְקָדְשָׁהּ
וְנָסוּ הַצְּלָלִים: וְהַעֲלֵה אוֹר שִׁמְשָׁהּ

בְּשִׁירָה קִדְּמוּךָ   יְדִידִים רוֹמְמוּךָ
אֲדֹנָי בָּאֵלִים: מִי־כָמֹכָה 20

77

SABBATH PEACE

To love of thee I drink my cup—
Peace to thee, peace, O Seventh Day!

Six days of work are like thy slaves,
While toiling through them, full of restlessness,
All of them seem to me but as a few days,
For the love I have to thee, O day of my delight!

Job 7.4.
Gen. 29.20.

I go forth on the first day to do my work,
To set in order the next Sabbath day's array:
For God hath placed the blessing there:
Thou alone art my portion for all my toil.

The lamp for my holy day is from the light of
mine Holy One;
The sun and stars are jealous of my sun.
What care I for the second day or the third?
Let the fourth day hide his lights—

77

שלום לך יום השביעי

‏— — — — | — — — —

אֶשְׁתָּה גְבִיעִי   עַל־אַהֲבָתָךְ
יוֹם הַשְּׁבִיעִי: שָׁלוֹם לְךָ שָׁלוֹם

לְךָ כַּעֲבָדִים   שֵׁשֶׁת יְמֵי מַעֲשֶׂה
אֶשְׁבַּע נְדָדִים   אִם־אֶעֱבֹד בָּהֶם
יָמִים אֲחָדִים   כֻּלָּם בְּעֵינַי הֵם   5
יוֹם שַׁעֲשׁוּעִי: מֵאַהֲבָתִי בָּךְ

לַעֲשׂוֹת מְלָאכָה   אֵצֵא בְּיוֹם רִאשׁוֹן
הַמַּעֲרָכָה   לַעֲרֹךְ לְיוֹם שַׁבָּת
שָׁם הַבְּרָכָה   כִּי הָאֱלֹהִים שָׁם
מִכָּל־יְגִיעִי: אַתָּה לְבַד חֶלְקִי   10

מְאוֹר קָדְשִׁי   מָאוֹר לְיוֹם קָדְשִׁי
קָנְאוּ לְשִׁמְשִׁי   שֶׁמֶשׁ וְכוֹכָבִים
אוֹ לַשְּׁלִישִׁי   מַה־לִּי לְיוֹם שֵׁנִי
יוֹם הָרְבִיעִי: יַסְתִּיר מְאֹרוֹתָיו

I hear a herald of good tidings from the fifth
    day forth:
To-morrow cometh fresh life for my soul!
The morning for my labour, the evening for
    my freedom;
I shall be summoned to the table of my King,
    my Shepherd!

I find upon the sixth day my soul rejoicing,
For there draweth nigh to me the time of rest;
Albeit I go about, a wanderer, to find relief,
At even I forget all my weariness and wander-
    ing.

How sweet to me the time between the lights—
To see the face of Sabbath, with mien renewed!
O come with apples, bring ye many raisin
    cakes—
This is the day of my rest, this my love, my
    friend.

I will sing to thee, O Sabbath, songs of love;
So it befitteth thee, for thou art a day of
    enjoyments,
A day of pleasures, yea, of banquets three,
Pleasure at my table, pleasure of my couch.

מִיוֹם חֲמִישִׁי	אֶשְׁמַע מְבַשֵּׂר טוֹב
נֶפֶשׁ לְנַפְשִׁי	כִּי־מָחֳרָת יִהְיָה
עֶרֶב לְחָפְשִׁי	בֹּקֶר לְעָבְדָתִי
מַלְכִּי וְרוֹעִי:	קָרוּא אֱלֵי שֻׁלְחַן

15

נַפְשִׁי שְׂמֵחָה	אָמְצָא בְיוֹם שִׁשִּׁי
עֵת הַמְּנוּחָה	כִּי־קָרְבָה אֵלַי
לִמְצֹא רְוָחָה	אִם נָע וָנָד אֵלֵךְ
נוֹדִי וְנוֹעִי:	עֶרֶב וְאֶשְׁכַּח כָּל־

20

בֵּין הַשְּׁמָשׁוֹת	מַה־נָּעֲמָה לִּי עֵת
פָּנִים חֲדָשׁוֹת	לִרְאוֹת פְּנֵי שַׁבָּת
הַרְבּוּ אֲשִׁישׁוֹת	בֹּאוּ בְתַפּוּחִים
דּוֹדִי וְרֵעִי:	זֶה יוֹם מְנוּחָי זֶה

25

שִׁירֵי יְדִידוֹת	אָשִׁיר לְךָ שַׁבָּת
אַתְּ יוֹם חֲמָדוֹת	כִּי־יָאֲתָה לָךְ כִּי
שָׁלֹשׁ סְעוּדוֹת	יוֹם תַּעֲנוּגִים גַּם
תַּעֲנוּג יְצוּעִי:	תַּעֲנוּג לְשֻׁלְחָנִי

30

78

A CAMPING PLACE

Fair and good it is to hold a camping place
    within Thine house,
For the people in whose midst Thy name doth
    rest;

That Name whose dwelling is the infinite space—
    though He
Isa. 57,15; 53,7. Is found within the contrite heart and with
    the humble man.

And heaven's heights cannot contain Him,
    even though
He came down upon Sinai and abode in a bush.

His way is very near and it is very far,
For all that He doeth is for the sake of all
    that is, and for His own sake.

Lo, upon my heart is a thought from my God;
Yea, also upon my tongue is an answer from
    the Lord.

78

בביתך מחנה
רשות

‒ ‒ | ‒ ∪ ‒ | ‒ ‒ ‒ | ‒ ∪ ‒

יָפָה וְטוֹב לָאָחוֹ בְּבֵיתְךָ מַחֲנֶה
לְעָם אֲשֶׁר שִׁמְךָ בְּקִרְבָּם יַחֲנֶה

הַשֵּׁם אֲשֶׁר שָׁכְנוֹ בְּרוּם עוֹלָם וְהוּא
נִמְצָא בְּלֵב דַּכָּא וְעָם אִישׁ נַעֲנֶה

וּשְׁמֵי מְרוֹמִים לֹא יְכִילוּהוּ וְאִם
יָרַד עֲלֵי סִינַי וְשָׁכַן בַּסְּנֶה

דַּרְכוֹ מְאֹד קָרְבָה וְלִמְאֹד רָחֲקָה
כִּי כֹל אֲשֶׁר פָּעַל לְיֵשׁ וּלְמַעֲנֶה

הֵן עַל־לְבָבִי מֵאֱלֹהַי מַחֲשָׁב
גַּם עַל־לְשׁוֹנִי מֵאֲדֹנָי מַעֲנֶה:

5

10

79

NATURE AND LAW[1]

(For rhymed version see page 172)

The words of God are pure; they are more
    precious than rubies;
They are wrapped up in hearts, they are
    bound up in souls.

Weary are all words with fervent pursuit after
    His praises,
For what hath one of numbered days to do
    with His infinite eternities?
As clouds above the dust, so high above him
    are God's ways.

How can understanding that is deficient and
    reason that is cut short
Grasp the ways of might, the high, the im-
    pregnable?

Be silent before Him, each that speaketh of Him,
    and perish his thought!
Only about His works let him frame song, let
    him ply his tongue;
Yea, concerning the law of His mouth let him
    lift his voice and make loud his throat.[2]

[1] Referred to by Zunz as a *Piyuṭ* for the 1st day of
Pentecost. It occurs in the Avignon ritual and others.

[2] The liturgies read these two lines thus:

אך במפעליו יחבר קול וירחיב את גרונו
ובדברי שיר ינבר פיו ויאריך את לשונו.

See rhymed version.

79

אמרות האל טהרות

מאורה

‏‎– – ◡ – | – – ◡ – | – – ◡ – | – – ◡ – | – ‏‎

מִפְּנִינִים הֵם יְקָרוֹת	אִמְרוֹת הָאֵל טְהֹרוֹת
בַּנְּפָשׁוֹת הֵם קְשׁוּרוֹת:	בַּלְּבָבוֹת הֵם צְרוּרוֹת
מִדְּלִק אַחַר שְׁבָחָיו	יָגְעוּ כָּל־הַדְּבָרִים
אַחֲרֵי נֶצַח נְצָחָיו	מַה־לְּבָךְ יָמִים סְפוּרִים
גָּבְהוּ מֶנּוּ אֲרָחָיו	כַּשְּׁחָקִים מֵעֲפָרִים
וּתְבוּנוֹת הַקְּצָרוֹת	מַה־לְּדֵעוֹת הַחֲסֵרוֹת
הַגְּבֹהַת הַבְּצֻרוֹת:	לָאֱחֹז דַּרְכֵי גְבוּרוֹת
בּוֹ, וְאָבַד רַעְיוֹנוֹ	הַס לְפָנָיו כָּל־מְדַבֵּר
שִׁיר וְיַאֲרִיךְ אֶת־לְשׁוֹנוֹ	אַךְ בְּמִפְעָלָיו יְחַבֵּר
קוֹל וְיָרִים אֶת־גְּרוֹנוֹ	גַּם בְּתוֹרַת פִּיו יְנַבֵּר

5

10

Tongues be giving forth speech, extolling,
    crowning;
Souls be glorifying, now to praise, and now to
    teach.[1]

Micah 6,6. But wherewith shall I bow down and be worthy
    to come before the Lord?[2]
Ps. 42,5. Shall I lead the procession to the house of God
    with calves for mine offering?
Will He say: I will deliver them from the
    grave; I will be a father to My children?

All the lands, behold, are alien;[3] so that one
    cannot bring an offering that is pure;
O build the chiefest city;[4] be Thou pleased as
    with oblation from her courts.

Isa. 19,6. Emptied is wisdom and dried up from the
    hearts of Kalkol and Darda:[5]
All that they have known[6] and thought
    is not as He thinketh and knoweth.
His works are too strong, too many, for the
    searching out of wisdom and reason.

His untold marvels, day by day, multiplying
    and bearing fruit—
Ps. 71,15. These give unceasingly songs to Him, knowing
    not their numbers. [7]

---

[1] The liturgies read here: בֵּין לְהָבִין וּלְהוֹרוֹת.

[2]   ”   ”   ”   ”   וַאֲדַבֵּר לַאֲדֹנָי.

[3]   ”   ”   ”   ”   .. הֵן אֲרָצוֹת כָּל לְזָרוֹת.

[4]   ”   ”   ”   ”   תִּבְנֶה רֵאשִׁית עִירוֹת.

[5] Wise men of the east. See I Kings 5,11.

[6] The liturgies read יֵמוּ for יָדְעוּ.

[7]   ”   ”   ”   סְדוּרוֹת for סְפוּרוֹת.

הַלְשֹׁנוֹת מַאֲמִירוֹת   מַעֲרִיצוֹת מַעֲטִירוֹת
הַנְּשָׁמוֹת מַאֲדִירוֹת   בֵּין לְהוֹדוֹת בֵּין לְהוֹרוֹת:

וּבְמָה אִכַּף אֲקַדֵּם   אֶזְכֶּה לִפְנֵי אֲדֹנָי
בֵּית אֱלֹהִים הָאֲדַדֵּם   בַּעֲגָלִים קָרְבָּנִי
15   מִשְׁאוֹל יֹאמַר וְאִפְדֵּם   אֶהְיֶה כָאָב לְבָנָי

כָּל־אֲרָצוֹת הֵן לְזָרוֹת   מִבְּלִי הַקְרִיב טְהוֹרוֹת
תִּבָּנֶה רֹאשׁ הָעֲיָרוֹת   תַּחֲפֹץ שַׁי בַּעֲזָרוֹת:

דָּלֲלוּ חָכְמוֹת וְחָרְבוּ   מִלֵּב כַּלְכֹּל וְדַרְדַּע
כֹּל אֲשֶׁר יָדְעוּ וְחָשְׁבוּ   לֹא כְּמוֹ חָשַׁב וְיָדַע
20   מַעֲשָׂיו עָצְמוּ וְרָבוּ   מֵחֲקֹר חָכְמָה וּמַדָּע

נִפְלְאוֹתָיו לֹא סְפוּרוֹת   יוֹם לְיוֹם רַבּוֹת וּפֵרוֹת
יִתְּנוּ תָמִיד זְמִרוֹת   לוֹ, וְלֹא יָדְעוּ סְפֹרוֹת:

Behold clear witnesses are Thine:　they fill
　　every mountain and hill;
For upon every creature's form there is of God
　　a seal and a token,
And the shining of all the lights—the shining
　　of seven for seven.

Even as He made of the seven lamps seven
　　constellations,
So maketh He men's eyes luminaries to look
　　upon the Light.

הָאֵלֶךְ עֵדִים בְּרוּרִים   מָלְאוּ כָל־הַר וָגֶבַע
כִּי בְכָל־צוּרוֹת יְצוּרִים   יֵשׁ לְאֵל חוֹתָם וָטֶבַע
זֹהֲרֵי כָל־הַמְּאוֹרִים   זָהֲרֵי שֶׁבַע לְשֶׁבַע   25

כַּאֲשֶׁר שֶׁבַע מְאֹרוֹת   שָׁם לְשֶׁבַע הַמְּנוֹרוֹת
שָׁם לְעֵינַיִם מְאִירוֹת   לַחֲזוֹת אֶת־הַמְּאֹרוֹת:

80

SLEEPER WITH HEART AWAKE
(For rhymed version see page 174)

O Sleeper, with heart awake, burning and
    tempest-tossed,
Go forth now and shake thyself, and walk in
    the light of My face.

Num. 24,17.   Arise, ride on and prosper: there shall come
    forth a star for thee,
And he who lay down in the dungeon shall
    go up to the summit of Sinai.

Let not their soul exult which say: Condemned
Is Zion; for lo! My heart is there, and Mine
    eyes are there.

I reveal Me and I hide Me; I am angry, I am
    appeased;
Who shall have pity upon my children except-
    ing I myself?

80

יָשֵׁן וְלִבּוֹ עֵר

רשות

‏— — — ◡ — —

בּוֹעֵר וּמִשְׁתָּעֵר	יָשֵׁן וְלִבּוֹ עֵר
וּלְכָה בְּאוֹר פָּנָי	צֵא־נָא וְהִנָּעֵר
דַּרְכָּךְ לְךָ כּוֹכָב	קוּמָה צְלַח וּרְכַב
עָלָה לְרֹאשׁ סִינָי	וַאֲשֶׁר בְּבוֹר שָׁכַב
הָאֹמְרִים תָּאֲשָׁם	אַל־תַּעֲלוֹז נַפְשָׁם
לְבִי וְשָׁם עֵינָי	צִיּוֹן וְהִנֵּה שָׁם
אָקְצֹף וְאֶעְתַּר	אָגֵל וְאָסְתַּר
מִנִּי עֲלֵי בָנָי:	מִי יַחֲמֹל יוֹתֵר

5

RHYMED TRANSLATIONS

2

ODE TO ZION

Zion, wilt thou not ask if peace's wing
  Shadows the captives that ensue thy peace,
Left lonely from thine ancient shepherding?

Lo! west and east and north and south—
    world-wide—
  All those from far and near, without sur-
    cease,
Salute thee: Peace and Peace from every side;

And Peace from him that from the captive's
    fount
  Of tears, is giving his like Hermon's dew,
And longing but to shed them on thy mount.

I with the jackal's wail have mourned thee
    long,
  But dreaming of thine own restored anew
I am a harp to sound for thee thy song.

My heart to Bethel sorely yearneth yet,
  Peniel and Mahanaim; yea, where'er
In holy concourse all thy pure ones met.

There the Shekhinah dwelt; to thee was given
   Thy Maker's Presence when He opened there
The gates of thee toward the gates of Heaven.

And only glory from the Lord was thine
   For light; and moon and stars and sunshine
      waned,
Nor gave more light unto thy light divine.

O I would choose but for my soul to pour
   Itself where then the Spirit of God remained
Outpoured upon thy chosen ones of yore.

Thou art the royal house; thou art the throne
   Of God; and how come slaves to sit at last
Upon the thrones which were thy lords' alone?

Would I were wandering in those places dear
   Where God revealed Himself in ages past,
Showing His light to messenger and seer!

And who will make me wings that I may fly,
   That I may take my broken heart away
And lay its ruins where thy ruins lie?

Prostrate upon thine earth, I fain would thrust
   Myself, delighting in thy stones, and lay
Exceeding tender hold upon thy dust.

Yea, more, at Hebron, by the tombs in her
   Of mine own fathers, I would stand and gaze
In wonder at thy chosen sepulchre;

And pass into thy forest and incline
   To Carmel, and would stand in Gilead's ways
And marvel at that distant mountain thine—[1]

Thy Mount Abarim and thy Mountain Hor,
   There where the two great luminaries sleep
Which were thy teachers and thy lights before.

The life of souls thine air is; yea, and thou
   Hast purest myrrh for grains of dust; and
      deep
With honey from the comb thy rivers flow.

Sweet to my soul 'twould be to wander bare
   And go unshod in places waxen waste—
Desolate since thine oracles were there;

Where thine Ark rested, hidden in thine heart,
   And where, within, thy Cherubim were
      placed
Which in thine inmost chambers dwelt apart.

I will cut off and cast away my crown
   Of locks, and curse the season which pro-
      faned
In unclean land the crowns which were thine
      own.

   [1] See note in prose version.

How shall it any more be sweet to me
  To eat or drink, while dogs all unrestrained
Thy tender whelps devouring I must see?

Or how shall light of day at all be sweet
  Unto mine eyes, while still I see them killed—
Thine eagles—caught in ravens' mouths for
    meat?

O cup of sorrow! gently! let thy stress
  Desist a little! for my reins are filled
Already, and my soul with bitterness.

I, calling back Oholah's memory,
  Drink thine hot poison; and remembering
Oholibah, I drain the dregs of thee.

Zion!   O perfect in thy beauty! found
  With love bound up, with grace encompass-
    ing,
With thy soul thy companions' souls are
    bound:

They that rejoice at thy tranquillity,
  And mourn the wasteness of thine overthrow
And weep at thy destruction bitterly;

They from the captive's pit, each one that
    waits

Panting towards thee; all they bending low,
Each one from his own place, towards thy
    gates;

The flocks of all thy multitudes of old
    That, sent from mount to hill in scattered
      flight,
Have yet forgotten nevermore thy fold;

That take fast, clinging hold upon thy skirt,
    Striving to grasp the palm-boughs on thine
      height,
To come to thee at last with strength begirt.

Shinar and Pathros—nay, can these compare
    With thee in state?   And can thy purity,
And can thy light be like the vain things
      there?

And thine anointed—who among their throng
    Compareth?   Likened unto whom shall be
Levites and seers and singers of thy song?

Lo! it shall pass, shall change, the heritage,
    Of vain-crowned kingdoms; not all time
      subdues
Thy strength; thy crown endures from age to
      age.

Thy God desired thee for a dwelling-place;
  And happy is the man whom He shall
      choose,
And draw him nigh to rest within thy space.

Happy is he that waiteth:—he shall go
  To thee, and thine arising radiance see
When over him shall break thy morning glow;

And see rest for thy chosen; and sublime
  Rejoicing find amid the joy of thee
Returned unto thine olden youthful time.

8

ON THE WAY TO JERUSALEM

Beautiful height! O joy! the whole world's
    gladness!
  O great King's city, mountain blest!
My soul is yearning unto thee—is yearning
    From limits of the west.

The torrents heave from depths of mine heart's
    passion,
  At memory of thine olden state,
The glory of thee borne away to exile,
    Thy dwelling desolate.

And who shall grant me, on the wings of
    eagles,
  To rise and seek thee through the years,
Until I mingle with thy dust beloved,
    The waters of my tears?

I seek thee, though thy King be no more in
    thee,
  Though where the balm hath been of old—
Thy Gilead's balm—be poisonous adders
    lurking,
    Winged scorpions manifold.

Shall I not to thy very stones be tender?
  Shall I not kiss them verily?
Shall not thine earth upon my lips taste
    sweeter
  Than honey unto me?

33

TO THE BRIDEGROOM

Rejoice, O young man, in thy youth,
  And gather the fruit thy joy shall bear,
Thou and the wife of thy youth,
  Turning now to thy dwelling to enter there.

Glorious blessings of God, who is One,
  Shall come united upon thine head;
  Thine house shall be at peace from dread,
Thy foes' uprising be undone.
  Thou shalt lay thee down in a safe retreat;
  Thou shalt rest, and thy sleep be sweet.

In thine honour, my bridegroom, prosper and
      live;
  Let thy beauty arise and shine forth fierce;
  And the heart of thine enemies God shall
      pierce,
And the sins of thy youth will He forgive,
  And bless thee in increase and all thou shalt
      do,
  When thou settest thine hand thereto.

And remember thy Rock, Creator of thee,
  When the goodness cometh which He shall
      bring;
  For sons out of many days shall spring,
And e'en as thy days thy strength shall be.
  Blessèd be thou when thou enterest,
  And thy going out shall be blest.

'Mid the perfect and wise shall thy portion lie,
  So thou be discreet where thou turnest thee;
  And thine house shall be builded immovably,
And "Peace" thou shalt call, and God shall
     reply;
  And peace shall be thine abode; and sealed
  Thy bond with the stones of the field.

Thy glory shall rise, nor make delay;
  And thee shall He call and choose; and thy
     light
In the gloom, in the darkness of the night,
Then shall break forth like the dawn of day;
  And out from the shining light of the morn
  Shall the dew of thy youth be born.

38

FORSAKEN

(The Hebrew text is translated from an Arabic song)

I am of little worth, and poor, apart
   From him, my glory; and amid the years
My form grows like a shadow; till my heart
   Is old, but not by my years' number; lo,
My witnesses:—the number of the years
   Of this my sojourning.   Nay, but I grow
So old in his forsaking.—If in truth
   He shall come back to me amid the years,
Then shall come back to me with him my youth.

47

HAST THOU FORGOTTEN?

My Love! hast Thou forgotten
  Thy rest
  Upon my breast?
And wherefore hast Thou sold me
To be enslaved for aye?
Have I not followed Thee upon the way
Of olden time within a land not sown?
Lo! Seir and Mount Paran—nor these alone—
  Sinai and Sin—yea these
  Be all my witnesses.

For Thee my love was ever,
  And mine
  Thy grace divine;
And how hast Thou apportioned
My glory away from me?
Thrust unto Seir, pursued, sent forth to flee
Until Kedar, nor suffered to abide;
Within the Grecian fiery furnace tried;
  Afflicted, weighed with care,
  With Media's yoke to bear—

And is there any to redeem but Thee?
Or other captive with such hope above?
O give Thy strength to me,
For I give Thee my love!

60

VISION OF GOD

To meet the fountain of true life I run;
Of this so vain and empty life I tire.
To see my King's face is my sole desire;
   Beside Him have I fear or dread of none.

O that a dream might hold Him in its bond!
I would not wake; nay, sleep should ne'er
    depart.
Would I might see His face within my heart!
   Mine eyes would never ask to look beyond.

62

WONDERFUL IS THY LOVE

Let my sweet song be pleasing unto Thee—
  The incense of my praise—
O my Belovèd that art flown from me,
  Far from mine errant ways!
(But I have held the garment of His love,
Seeing the wonder and the might thereof).
The glory of Thy name is my full store—
My portion for the toil wherein I strove:
Increase the sorrow:—I shall love but more!
  Wonderful is Thy love!

66

THE LORD IS MY PORTION

Servants of time, lo! these be slaves of slaves;
  But the Lord's servant hath his freedom
    whole.
Therefore, when every man his portion craves,
  "The Lord God is my portion," saith my
    soul.

69

UNTIL DAY AND NIGHT SHALL CEASE

Lo! sun and moon, these minister for aye;
   The laws of day and night cease nevermore:
Given for signs to Jacob's seed that they
   Shall ever be a nation—till these be o'er.
If with His left hand He should thrust away,
   Lo! with His right hand He shall draw them
     nigh.
Let them not cry despairing, nay, nor say:
   Hope faileth and our strength is near to die.
Let them believe that they shall be alway,
   Nor cease until there be no night nor day.

73

GOD IN ALL

O Lord, where shall I find Thee?
  All-hidden and exalted is Thy place;
And where shall I not find Thee?
  Full of Thy glory is the infinite space.

  Found near-abiding ever,
He made the earth's ends, set their utmost bar;
  Unto the nigh a refuge,
Yea, and a trust to those who wait afar.
  Thou sittest throned between the Cherubim,
  Thou dwellest high above the cloud-rack dim.
Praised by Thine hosts and yet beyond their
      praises
  Forever far exalt;
The endless whirl of worlds may not contain
      Thee,
  How, then, one temple's vault?

  And Thou, withal uplifted
O'er man, upon a mighty throne apart,
  Art yet forever near him,
Breath of his spirit, life-blood of his heart!
  His own mouth speaketh testimony true
  That Thou his Maker art alone; and who
Shall fear Thee not, for lo! upon their shoulders
  Thy yoke divinely dread!
Who shall forbear to cry to Thee, That givest
  To all their daily bread?

Longing I sought Thy presence;
Lord, with my whole heart did I call and pray,
  And going out toward Thee,
I found Thee coming to me on the way;
  Yea, in Thy wonders' might as clear to see
  As when within the shrine I looked for Thee.
Who saith he hath not seen Thee?   Lo! the
      heavens
  And all their host, aflame
With glory, show Thy fear with speech un-
      uttered,
  With silent voice proclaim.
  And can the Lord God truly—

God, the Most High—dwell here within man's
      breast?
  What shall he answer, pondering—
Man, whose foundations in the dust do rest?
  For Thou art holy, dwelling 'mid the praise
  Of them that waft Thee worship all their
      days.
Angels adoring, singing of Thy wonder,
  Stand upon Heaven's height;
And Thou, enthroned o'erhead, all things
      upholdest
  With everlasting might.

76

A NEW SONG

The day the saved of God
Traversed the deep dryshod,
Then a new song
Sang Thy redeemèd throng.

Lo, sunken in deceit
The Egyptian daughter's feet,
The while, the Shulamite
Went shod in fair delight.[1]
Then a new song
Sang Thy redeemèd throng.

All that on Jeshurun gaze
Shall see him shrined in praise,[2]
For Jeshurun's God arose
Acclaimèd by his foes.
Then a new song
Sang Thy redeemèd throng.

Thy banners Thou wilt set
O'er those remaining yet,
And gather those forlorn
As gathering ears of corn.
Then a new song
Sang Thy redeemèd throng.

[1] See note 1 in prose version.
[2] See note 3 in prose version.

These that have come to Thee
Under Thy seal to be,
They from the birth are Thine,
Bound by a holy sign.
Then a new song
Sang Thy redeemèd throng.

Their token show to all
Whose eyes upon them fall:
Lo, on their garment's hem
The fringe ordained for them!
Then a new song
Sang Thy redeemèd throng.

For whom then are they sealed?
Let truth now be revealed:
Whose is the seal, and who
Shall claim the thread of blue?
Then a new song
Sang Thy redeemèd throng.

Ah, take her as of yore,
And cast her forth no more;
Let sunlight crown her day
And shadows flee away.
Then a new song
Sang Thy redeemèd throng.

For Thy belovèd throng
Still come to Thee with song,
Singing with one accord:
Now who is like Thee 'mid the gods, O Lord!
Still Thy redeemèd throng
Sing a new song.

79

NATURE AND LAW

The words of God are pure
And precious more than gems in fair display;
They are bound up in hearts for ever, yea,
    In souls are held secure.

All speech grows weary in pursuit that flies
    After His endless praise—
    For what hath one of numbered days
To do with infinite eternities?—
    As clouds above the dust, above him
        soar God's ways.

What of the mind cut short?
And reason that is lacking strength to know?
How should it grasp the way of power—so
    Impregnable a fort?

Silence before Him, all that speak of Him!
And perish all their thought!
    Only the works His hand hath wrought
Let them declare, and may their lips o'erbrim
With singing and their voice be loud with
        praises fraught.

Tongues be fulfilled of speech,
Exalting, crowning, telling o'er His praise;
Souls be extolling, still discerning ways
    To learn and tell and teach.

But how shall I all humbly seek the Lord?
  Oblation once I gave
  Within His house—and "From the grave"
He said, "I yet will lift them at My word,
  And I will be a father to the sons I save."

  But strange are all the lands;
One cannot bring a gift without alloy.
Rebuild the chiefest city!   Find Thy joy
  As once from holier hands.

Wisdom is withered that abode in state
  In hearts exceeding wise,
  For all they thought and did devise
Is other than He knoweth; yea, too great,
  Too many are His works for sight of wisdom's
    eyes.

  His wonders manifold
Bring daily marvels new in fruitful throngs.
These give to Him, unceasing, only songs,
  In numbers all untold.

Behold, clear witnesses enough are Thine!
  All mountains under Heaven
  They fill; on every form is graven
The seal of God; and all about them shine
  The kindred lights in heaven and earth of
    stars twice seven.

  For seven in the height
There shine the seven lamps in earthly guise,
Given to so illume the earth-dimmed eyes
  To look upon His light.

80

SLEEPER, WITH HEART AWAKE

O Sleeper with heart that waketh,
  Burning and tempest-torn,
Go, shake thee, walk with My radiance
  Upon thee borne.

Rise up, ride on and prosper:
  A star shall guide thy quest,
Till he that lay down in the dungeon
  Reach Sinai's crest.

Let not their soul be joyful
  Which talk of Zion's despair,
For there My heart is ever,
  And Mine eyes are there.

I reveal Myself and I hide Me,
  I am wroth, I restrain the rod;
For who should pity My children
  But I, their God?

NOTES ON TEXT

להתעופף חמשים

Ll. 9–10 וְהָאָנְתָה] The ו signifies "since (thou still)", as in Gen. 26,27: ואתם שנאתם; similarly for הלא Halper reads ולא; I have called attention in the notes *ad loc.* to the fact that this is an unnecessary correction introduced by Luzzatto, in conflict with the testimony of the manuscript.

L. 27. וְיָמוּטוּ] Ḳal, comp. Deut. 32, 35 and Isa. 54,10; the irregular vowel is due to the intended homophony with the verbs in l. 28, but this stylistic effect would be lost if we read וְיִמּוֹטוּ with Halper.

L. 50. וּבַרְזִלֵּי אֲדָנִים] So Ms. Oxford 1970; Luzzatto, following MS. Oxford 1971, has וברזלי אבנים, for which Halper suggests וברזל ואבנים.

L. 62. הָעֲצָמִים] So in the manuscripts which I have used, with the masc. suffix on account of the following adjective; the reading העצמות, which Halper prefers, should be ascribed to the haste of a copyist, who undoubtedly was familiar with Ez. 37, 4.

L. 68. וְכִתְכַלָּת] So the manuscripts. The sense is: He

who observes the night sees a Mooress (the black‑
ness of the night) in a dress interwoven with gold
threads, and purple blue plains (sky and sea),
set with jewels (the stars in heaven and their
reflection in the mirror of the sea); comp. the fol‑
lowing verses and שהתכלת דומה לים ויום דומה לרקיע
in Soṭa 17a, Ḥul. 89a, Men. 43b. I consider
Edelmann's reading וּבְתָכְלָת, preferred by Halper,
as a scribal error or a misprint.

Ll. 73-74. עֲדִי יָם עֲדִי לָיִל] Halper corrects and reads עֲדָיִים
for עֲדִי יִם, following MS. Amram against all
other texts, עֲלֵי לָיִל for עֲדֵי לָיִל. The obvious
correction עדיים is found also in S. Joseph, *Gibeat
Saul*, p. 108, who, however, retains עדי ליל, though
apparently vocalizing it עֲדִי לָיִל. I cannot imagine
that the poet wishes to designate sky and sea as
ornaments of the night, nor do I find an analogy
to this daring picture in any other poet. As
long therefore as there is not a better reading or
a MS. confirmation of this emendation, I shall
cling to the traditional text, of which it can by no
means be said that it "makes no sense". The
poet says, while applying עדי to space and time:
"as far as the sea stretches, as long as the night
lasts—smooth watery mirror and clear celestial
canopy". This thought is by no means unworthy
of expression.

8

יפה נוף משוש תבל

It is difficult to establish definitely the metre
of this poem. I have previously construed it
as Baṣiṭ (*Diwan* and שער השיר, p. 96) and hence
vocalized לְךָ in l. 2; later I abandoned this view
(without giving up my theory with reference to
anacrusis; comp. note to No. 68, l. 10, further
below) and saw in it a Ṭawil, whence I vocalized
לָךְ (מבחר השירה העברית, p. קפג) without introducing
any other changes, because I believe that *faʻlun*
is admissible for *faʻulun* ($-$ $-$ for $\smile$ $\smile$ $-$); comp.
my *Studien zu den Dichtungen Jeh. ha-Levis*, p. 26,
n. 2; comp. also No. 9 of this collection and the
note in *Diwan*, I, 137. Halper ("*The Scansion*,
etc." in *JQR.*, N. S., IV, 169ff.) likewise takes the
metre for Ṭawil, but he does not admit a change
of metrical feet, preferring to change the text in
six places. These changes I consider quite grat-
uitous. It is inconceivable to me how a connoisseur
of language and poetry of Dr. Halper's rank could
assume that Halevi said: וְאִם אֵין בָּךְ מְלָכַיִךְ (comp.
the vocalization and word-order in Jer. 8,19).
מְלָכַיִךְ is amorphous and anomalous, having no
analogy in Scripture; the reference to Eccles. 10,17
is without importance, for אַשְׁרֵיךְ is sing. despite
the י, but even if we follow Ibn Gikatilla in declar-

ing it a plural, then it is just a plural which by exception appears vocalized as a sing.; but I find no evidence at all for a suffixed noun vocalized half as a sing. and half as a plural.

26
למבחר החתנים

Ll. 2–3. יְחַם—יְחַם], comp. note *ad loc.* (*Diwan*, II, notes, p. 13); according to the correction introduced here (following the reading of Saphir quoted by Harkavy, III, 186) the sense is as follows: "The friend, from whom they (the friends gathered at the wedding feast) are far away, wishes to see them with his eyes, but his heart sees them as if they were standing before him."

32
בת שחר

L. 2. The reading given seems to me better than that of Davidson: וּלְקוֹל שִׁירָה נָעוֹרָה.

L. 8. מְרָקְחִים] Davidson: מרחקים.

L. 13. מְדַּדִיךָ] Davidson: הַיּוֹם—מְדֹוָדִיךָ Davidson: כיום (MS. ביום).

L. 15. וְיֻשְׁלָם] So Davidson, better than ישלים of my archetype.

L. 18. עָפְרַת נָוֶה] better than Davidson: עפרה נוה.

Ll. 19–22. I follow Davidson's better readings, down to

אֵת, which is wanting in his archetype and for which he substitutes נָא. The sense is given in my notes to the *Diwan*, II, 34; the linguistic difficulties, which called forth my remark: וכונת הבית פשוטה בכללה ולא בפרטיה, are thus removed.

L. 25. בָּרָה] Davidson: יוֹנָה.

L. 26. שַׁחַר פָּנֶיהָ שֶׁחַר] This is Davidson's reading; the sense is: "he who sees (literally: searches) her face sees the splendour of the stars". This reading is more interesting than that of the *Diwan:* שַׁחַר פָּנֶיהָ שַׁחֵר, which is adopted in the translation.

L. 27. אֶל] So also Davidson; Ex. 25,37: עַל.

33

שמח בחור

L. 18. תֹם] The manuscripts have: תֹם ובין; perhaps we should read בֵּין מְתַי תֹם.

35

עדי עש יעופף

L. 1. יְרַדְּפוּנִי]. The vocalization יָרְדְּפוּנִי suggested by Halper (*JQR.*, *l. c.*, p. 164 and 206) would be admissible, but since the given vocalization is corroborated in the Bible (Ps. 7,6) there is no ground for the assumption that the poet employed poetic license *metri causa*.

38

לפרוד

L. 1. וְדָלוֹתִי] *Plene* (following Ps. 142,7), because we
usually find it so in these forms; hence also נְקַלֹּתִי
(despite 2 Sam. 6,22), in order to emphasize the
inner rhyme visually. S. Joseph (*l. c.*, p. 300)
would like to write נְקַלֹּתִי, but then וְדַלֹּתִי (Ps. 116,6)
would also have to be preferred, as in Kämpf,
Nichtandal. Poesie, II, 226.—לְפְרוֹד] In Edelmann,
גנזי אקספרד p. 25, the reading כפרוד is an error due
to haste (for the manuscript underlying it, MS.
Oxford 1970, exhibits our reading), which S.
Joseph would like to retain. The fortunately
preserved Arabic text (ממא הנרת), is against it.

L. 6. וְשׁוּבֵנִי] I accept this correction of Joseph.

39

בך הגביר יצחק

L. 8. מִתְעַנְּגָה and מְתָפַּנֶּקֶת] refer as well to אֶרֶץ (l. 1) as
to בַּת (l. 7), and there is no cause for reading in
l. 7 בִּלְבוּשׁ instead of בְּלָבוֹשׁ (as suggested by Joseph
l. c., p. 189).

L. 10. סָבִיבָיהָ כְּסוּת] So three manuscripts, among them
the one used by Edelmann; it is therefore again
an error of haste when in גנזי אקספרד, p. 41, he
prints סביבה. S. Joseph corrected the text—before

the reading of the manuscripts was known—into סְבִיבָה הַכְּסוּת, which is possible but cannot be maintained against the evidence of three manuscripts. The explanation which he offers is very far from sound, as in general he tries to read into the poem thoughts which are not contained in it (comp. for instance, his forced construction of ll. 23–30). I cannot deal with this matter here at greater length.

L. 26. זוֹרָקֵת] has reference to עָב in the preceding line (femin. 1 Kings, 18,44.)

L. 48. מַעְתָּקֵת] comp. my note *ad loc.*, but it is possible that the poet wants to have it understood in the sense of עָתָק (comp. Job, 21,7 and elsewhere, further Ibn Ganaḥ *s. v.*): she intones a doubly powerful song. Joseph (and also Bacher) would like to read מַמְתָּקֵת, but since this word occurs above, l. 28, in a rhyme, he tries to force upon it there a sense (לשון עצה כלומר מתיעצת) which it has nowhere else, not even in the passage Ps. 55, 15 quoted by him as proof.

L. 56. מַחֲנֶה] Joseph wants to read מַחֲנָה, which is possible. To emend וּלְךְ into וּבְךְ I consider unnecessary; comp. הַזְעֵק-לִי 2 Sam. 20,4.

L. 58. וּלְתַעֲלָמָה] without Mappik, as found in some editions of Job 28,11; other editions exhibit there וְתַעֲלָמָה, but this reading would lead to misinter-

pretations, such as may be seen in Joseph, p.
196, who construes Edelmann's slips of the pen
(ולתעלמיה מורקת p. 41: ננזי אקספרד) as readings and
endeavors to defend them.

40

שמואל הנגיד

L. 1. מִגְזָרִים] with Dagesh in the נ, as Nah. 3,17.

L. 14. בֵּין] Joseph, p. 199, suggests בבין *metri causa*, after
having denied in a note on the preceding page
that the poem has any metre.

L. 22. וְנִהְים] Participle Niphʻal; Joseph, p. 199, suggests
נוהים (Ḳal) despite the fact that the only passage
where the verb נהה occurs in the sense intended
here (1 Sam. 7,2) exhibits the Niphʻal.

L. 29 אֲנִי] Four syllables are found in hemistichs else-
where (even 1a); Joseph's suggestion to read אָנִי
is not acceptable.

L. 32 וְחָיֵי] Joseph (p. 200) wants to emend it to ומחיה (pro-
bably so for ומחיי of the edition), by analogy with
מרפא, but a noun corresponds with a noun, not a
participle.

41

לנד משה

L. 55. חֲרָשִׁים] Following a correction by Ch. N. Bialik
in the second edition of the מבחר השירה העברית,

which is to appear soon; the difficulties of the verse are now removed.

L. 65. וְנָקַל] Participle, like the following וְנִדְמָה; נָקַל, as suggested by Joseph, would be a Perfect and out of place here.

52

ידע מכאבינו

L. 1. מַכְאֲבֵינוּ] So all the texts in keeping with Ex. 3,7; the rhyme requires מַכְאֲבַתֵינוּ, in which case the *Pathah furt.* of יָדַע would not be counted metrically.

68

כלה לך כלתה

L. 2 חִלְחָה] The ל without Dagesh, *metri causa*, as שֶׁלְחָה Ez. 17,7; 31,4 *et al.*

L. 10. וְנַפְשָׁה] with short syllable before the metre *Mustaf-ʿilun*, in spite of Halper's conclusions (*JQR., l. c.*, p. 169 and 183).

72

כי בא אור

L. 5. In the literal quotation of Bible verses the metre is neglected, as I have often pointed out. In this poem there is another instance in l. 9. In view of this the correction עָדֶי for עַד (Prov. 6,9) in l. 16 may be superfluous.

77

שלום לך יום השביעי

L. 6. ‏[שַׁעֲשׁוּעַי‎] This reading is better than מַרְגּוֹעַי, because
it does not force us to read a *Shewa quiescens*
as *Shewa mobile*.

L. 27. ‏[שִׁירֵי יְדִידוֹת‎] So in the Karaite Prayer Book (ed.
Wien 1854, vol. IV, p. ‏צב‎); ‏שִׁיר אֵל יְדִידוֹת‎ cannot
be explained; ‏שִׁיר יְדִידוֹת‎ (Halberstam in Luzzatto,
‏טל אורות‎, p. 2, n. 4) is against the metre; ‏שִׁיר הַיְדִידוֹת‎,
as found in some editions (so ‏שבחי אלהים‎, Oran 1885
p. ‏נ‎), can be looked upon only as an awkward
correction.

מקורות השירים

דיואן = דיואן רי"ה י"ל ע"י חיים בראדי.

שער = שער השיר להנ"ל.

מבחר = מבחר השירה העברית להנ"ל.

שד"ל = דיואן רי"ה י"ל ע"י שד"ל.

הרכוי = רבי יהודה הלוי קובץ שיריו ומליצותיו י"ל ע"י אברהם אליהו הרכוי.

----

16 דיואן ח"ב צד 175 סי' ט"ז (הערות צד 131).

17 דיואן ח"ב צד 180 סי' י"ח (הערות צד 133).

18 דיואן ח"ב צד 180 סי' י"ט (הערות צד 134).

19 דיואן ח"ב צד 182 סי' כ (הערות צד 136).

20 דיואן ח"ב צד 183 סי' כ"א (הערות צד 136).

21 דיואן ח"ב צד 183 סי' כ"ב (הערות צד 138).

22 דיואן ח"ב צד 184 סי' כ"ג (הערות צד 138); שער צד 96 סי' 83; מבחר צד קפ"ז סי' 9.

23 דיואן ח"ב צד 3 סי' א (הערות צד 3); מבחר צד קע"ח סי' 5.

24 דיואן ח"ב צד 7 סי' ד (הערות צד 7); שער צד 92 סי' 77; מבחר צד קע"ה סי' 1.

25 דיואן ח"ב צד 12 סי' ז (הערות צד 11).

26 דיואן ח"ב צד 13 סי' ט (הערות צד 13).

27 דיואן ח"ב צד 18 סי' ט"ו (הערות צד 18).

28 דיואן ח"ב צד 19 סי' ט"ז (הערות צד 19).

29 דיואן ח"ב צד 20 סי' י"ח (הערות צד 21); מבחר צד קע"ח סי' 3.

30 דיואן ח"ב צד 21 סי' כ (הערות צד 22).

31 דיואן ח"ב צד 29 סי' כ"ה (הערות צד 32).

32 דיואן ח"ב צד 29 סי' כ"ו (הערות צד 33). נדפס גם ע"י החו' ר"י דוידזאן על פי כ"י בעתון JQR. N.S., Vol. IV, p. 86 והוא מיחס אותו לר' יוסף בן צדיק. שהוא מחברו של השיר הבא אח"ז בכ"י. אולם ממה שנרשם על השיר שלאחריו "מנשה אחר לבן צדיק" יש ללמוד, שהשיר שלפנינו איננו לו, והמעתיק העתיק לעצמו שירים ממשוררים שונים שישרו בעיניו.

33 דיואן ח"ב צד 34 סי' ל"ד (הערות צד 39).

34 דיואן ח"ב צד 37 סי' ל"ו (הערות צד 41).

35 דיואן ח"ב צד 45 סי' מ"ו (הערות צד 49).

מפתח השירים על סדר הא"ב